Yankee Notions

ANNE CHISLETT

Playwrights Canada Press
Toronto

Playwrights Canada Press is the publishing imprint of
the Playwrights Union of Canada: 54 Wolseley St., 2nd fl.
Toronto, Ontario CANADA M5T 1A5
Tel: (416) 947-0201 Fax: (416) 947-0159

Playwrights Canada Press operates with the generous assistance of
The Canada Council - Writing and Publishing Section, and Theatre Section,
and the Ontario Arts Council.

Front cover: Oliver Dennis and Deborah Drakeford - Blyth Festival, 1992.
Front cover photo by James Hockings.
Edited and designed by Tony Hamill.

Canadian Cataloguing in Publication Data
Anne Chislett,
        Yankee notions
A play
ISBN 0-88754-497-5
I. Title.
PS8555.H58Y3 1993   C812'.54   C93-094718-5
PR9199.3.C55Y3   1993

First edition: August 1993
Printed and bound in Winnipeg, Manitoba, Canada.

Yankee Notions was origninally commissioned by the Stratford Festival Foundation under the artistic directorship of John Hirsch.

The play was first produced by Ryerson Theatre School. The first professional production opened at the Blyth Festival July 17, 1992.

Introduction by Damir Andrei

"Those who do not know their history are doomed to repeat it." Never had that dictum seemed truer than when I was directing the premiere of *Yankee Notions* at the Blyth Festival in June of 1992. Canadians seemed to be in a virtual state of rebellion against their governing elites, and their revolt culminated later that fall when they decisively rejected the Charlottetown Accord and repudiated the judgment of the political establishment. The analogies to the events of the Rebellion of 1837 were irresistible. Here again was a Tory government that had become dangerously removed from the ordinary citizen, that had ruined the economy through inept stewardship and punitive taxes, that seemed hell-bent on passing laws that disenfranchised ordinary Canadians, while rewarding the governing elite and their cronies. On our opening night, when Maria Wait tells her baby that even though the rebels have lost, "there'll be a next time...even if mama has to take up the gun and shoot all the Tories herself," there was a spontaneous ovation from the audience; generations later the situation and sentiments were all too familiar. For the Blyth audience, *Yankee Notions* was no longer an historical epic, but a play about all of us today, every Canadian who had despaired of our governing classes and wanted to strike a blow for change.

That so many of the issues bedeviling us today were fully formed problems in 1837 testifies to the strength of the repetitive patterns of political and economic relations which characterize our history, again and again. Knowing and understanding The Family Compact allows us insight into a host of Canadian realities, from the pork-barrelling of the Senate to the oligarchic, corporate cross-ownership of the Canadian economy. Yet we Canadians have been disenfranchised from our history through boring books and uninspired teaching. *Yankee Notions* is an 'alternative' history not only because it is the story of those who lost, but also because it's funny, moving, and inspiring.

Civil wars are often the crucible in which a state and its warring citizens discover who they really are. The victors will stamp their beliefs indelibly on the national culture, but the defeated will often remain, like ghost limbs on the body politic, an aching possibility of what might have been. They wait for future generations to regenerate the ideas and passions for which they were willing to kill and be killed. Often the passage of time is kind to them, certainly imbuing them with a romantic stature, but also sometimes proving them right and ahead of their time.

Of all wars, civil wars are certainly the most terrible. As a Canadian born in Croatia I fell that particularly keenly nowadays, as the Balkans has become a slaughterhouse. More than ever, I appreciate the Canadian tendency to endlessly discuss our differences, rather than using AK-47's to wipe them out. But violence has often been the precursor of a catalyst, of necessary social and political change. Just think of Oka. We owe are present stability, not to those who fought to preserve the status quo, but to those who fought for change, and often lost.

Why would a woman risk her family and her life for an idea? And what risky ideas might a conservative young lady use to save the lives of her family? Here is a story of civil rebellion, when some Canadians got so fed up with their political elites that they decided to get rid of them; a risky idea that still appeals.

June 20, 1993

The Characters

This suggested casting is arranged for 9 Equity and 2 non-equity actors*.

SARAH
MARIA
ANNIE,   doubles as EMMA, MRS. MOODIE
LIZZIE*   doubles as PEGGY, LADY MACNAB

ROBINSON   doubles as ONLOOKER
MACDONALD doubles as MESSENGER
DURHAM   doubles as BEN, ONLLOKER,
                   PIPER/FIDDLER
SAM   doubles as MACNAB, COUPER
ARTHUR   doubles as WHEELER, PURSER
LUKIN   doubles as HANGMAN
JAKE*   doubles as VICTIM, SERVANT to Robinson,
                   SAILOR on Durham's boat, FRENCH
                   PORTER, FOOTMAN to DURHAM,
                   MERRIT.

The SAILOR in Act Two, Scene Eleven may be any male voice, offstage.

N.B. MARIA is pronounced in the old fashioned way - MARIAH.

The Set

Yankee Notions calls for a unit structure, allowing easy movement and a good number of entrance options. The text frees the designer from the necessity of literally designating each location. Places to sit, i.e. steps or levels, would make changes easier. Set pieces should be kept small and easily portable. i.e. folding campaign desks and folding chairs, wooden writing boxes; a single elegant chair and butler's table for Castle St. Louis; a Plant or tree branch for the Garden of Beverley House. In the Blyth Festival production benches used in the boat scene were inverted to create piers for the following scenes.

The play works best if the set is divided as little as possible for different locations. All locations should "spill centre" allowing the action to flow over most of the stage. Scene headings are for rehearsal convenience. The action is never interrupted.

Playwright's Notes

Yankee Notions is a work of fiction based on a book called "The Wait Letters" published by Maria and Benjamin Wait in 1842, and a later book by the same title, edited by Mary Brown. The books tell the true story of a young rebel's adventures, and his wife's efforts to save his life. It also depicts early Canadian politics from the point of view of an articulate and highly opinionated twenty-five year old woman. Her account of Canada's formative years is much at odds with the history we learn in school.

Until Maria's book forced me to study the actual documents from the period, I believed that the Upper Canadian rebellion of 1837 began and ended with MacKenzie's farcical march down Yonge Street, and that government reaction was typically moderate and sensible. In fact, the rebels continued to fight well into the summer of 1838, and their battle against the United Empire Loyalist elite who dominated colonial life under British Governors was taken very seriously at the time. So was the threat of American intervention. There was considerable violence on both sides, and fear of civil war drove thousands of settlers from their homes.

Like most Canadians, I had received the impression that our history is one of dull evolution toward the rule of law and sound government, orchestrated by colourless old men in black coats. Yet the author of The Durham Report emerges from his family's correspondence as the wild, romantic character I've portrayed. The extent to which our heroines influenced him is my fiction, but there is documentation of the jurisdictional dispute with Sir George Arthur that resulted from His Lordship's efforts on behalf of Mrs. Wait and Miss Chandler. In Durham's papers there is a reference to the letter from Maria relating her (*Act Two*) encounter with Arthur. Moreover, after the events portrayed in *Yankee Notions*, while Durham was writing his Report from his death bed in Italy, his mother-in-law, the wife of Earl Gray, offered both her hospitality and her influence to the astonishing young woman recently arrived from Upper Canada.

Act One, Scene One

THE COURTYARD OF THE NIAGARA JAIL

The Town Clock begins to toll under the pre-show music, coming up as the music fades out, so that the tolling alone continues into the blackout.

Lights up on four anxious women. SARAH CHANDLER is a pretty seventeen-year old. Her dress is of good quality, but she is without bonnet or accessories. MARIA WAIT, who holds a baby in her arms, is twenty four. Her travel-worn clothes were never as stylish as SARAH's. ANNIE BEEMER, about fifty, and her teenage daughter, LIZZIE, are coarser in appearance.

Lights up on a scaffold or gallows' steps. The jailer, WHEELER, stands nearby. He is looking through a spy glass, hoping for something to appear in the distance.

SARAH (*addressing the audience*) Saturday, August twenty fifth, 1838. Niagara, Upper Canada.

WHEELER abandons his vigil.

WHEELER (*shouting to an offstage guard*) Bring'em out.

These are the words the women have been dreading.

SARAH (*a desperate appeal to WHEELER*) We were promised a reprieve. I swear we were.

WHEELER   Miss, I've held off as long as I could.

                 SARAH crosses back to ANNIE and
                 MARIA. Their eyes meet in silent despair.

MARIA   (*bitterly*) You were right, Sarah. The freest
                 parliament in the world wouldn't comfort me
                 now.

SARAH   Maria...(*making a dreadful confession*) You're not
                 to blame.

MARIA   They condemned him because of my letter. You
                 told me so yourself.

SARAH   Yes...but what I didn't tell you...they would
                 never have found your letter...or even known
                 about it...if I hadn't told them.

MARIA   (*an intake of breath*) You sold me out?

SARAH   (*nodding*) Your husband's death won't be your
                 fault. It will be mine.

                 MARIA stares at her a moment, then
                 turns her back. The HANGMAN enters
                 and mounts the scaffold.

LIZZIE   (*recognizing him*) Look! He's the wretch with
                 mouths to feed.

                 ANNIE kneels, indicating that LIZZIE
                 should kneel with her.

ANNIE   Child, it's time to say our prayers.

LIZZIE   But ain't he? Ain't he the same as last time?

                 The bell stops and the scene freezes. The
                 lighting changes to focus on SARAH
                 downstage.

SARAH (*looking at LIZZIE and picking up on her last line, to herself*) The last time. (*turning to address the audience*) The first time I stood in this spot and watched an execution. Before I'd met the woman I've since betrayed.

MARIA exits.

Before I discovered what it feels like to be betrayed. Before I believed the rebellion in Upper Canada could ever touch me. It was only three weeks ago.

ALL others exit. SARAH picks up a pre-set traveling bag and puts on a lace scarf and bonnet as she becomes an innocent young lady with high expectations.

Mama said the letter was a hoax! Yet another scoundrel trying to defraud us. After six months she'd given up hope, but I still clung to mine. All the way to Niagara the stage wheels repeated the message...Papa's been found! Papa's been found!

MACDONALD enters at the side of the stage. He is a tall, red-haired man in his early twenties. He's young enough to be shy socially and over-confident professionally.

MACDONALD (*addressing the audience*) Monday, August sixth. 1838. (*tapping his unreliable pocket watch and waiting for someone other than SARAH to arrive*)

SARAH (*uncertain*) Are you Mr. MacDonald?

MACDONALD (*incredulous*) You're Samuel Chandler's wife?

SARAH His daughter.

MACDONALD Oh...(*embarrassed*) pardon me.

SARAH	Where is he?
MACDONALD	(*hesitant*) Well...before we go into that... (*attempting to take her arm*)...my office is around the corner...
SARAH	Is Papa there?
MACDONALD	(*hesitating again*) I'm afraid not.
SARAH	(*pulling away her arm*) You wrote you knew his whereabouts?
MACDONALD	My note was to your mother. I didn't expect -- someone so young.
SARAH	I brought a reward if that's what you're worried about.
MACDONALD	No, no...You misunderstand. (*taking a breath*) Miss Chandler, I'm a qualified lawyer, and I can be of great service to your family.
SARAH	All I want is to find my father. Either take me to him...or...I'll go to a magistrate and charge you with fraud.
MACDONALD	(*stung*) Very well. The jail's around the corner.
SARAH	(*astonished*) The jail!
WHEELER	Bring'em out!

> *At the mention of "jail", the clock resumes tolling. Lights come up on the full stage. ANNIE and LIZZIE and two or three ONLOOKERS enter. The ONLOOKERS are in a party mood. ANNIE and LIZZIE pick up saying the Rosary, rattling off Hail Mary's without expression. WHEELER and a black-hooded HANGMAN lead out a victim who wears the jacket of the Patriot army. [blue, with two homemade white stars sewn on*

> *the breast. He should have a large*
> *blindfold or white hood]. They climb the*
> *gallows. [If the top of the gallows is out*
> *of the audience's sight, a dummy may be*
> *"hanged" instead of the actor]*

ANNIE
& LIZZIE   Holy Mary, Mother of God, pray for us sinners.

> *As the women pray, The ONLOOKERS*
> *hoot, jeer and sing to the tune of "Pop*
> *Goes the Weasel"*

ONLOOKERS   I tell a tale of Rebel Yank
To end his life of evil
There's but one step for the Yank to take
From the gallows to the devil.

ANNIE
& LIZZIE   Now and at the hour...

ONLOOKER 1   Dangle him slow, Ketch!

ONLOOKER 2   Make the bastard dance!

> *SARAH and MACDONALD enter the*
> *scene on the last stroke of the clock. A*
> *hush falls as we hear a drum roll, then a*
> *moment of complete silence.*

WHEELER   (*proclaiming*) God save the Queen.

> *The gallows trap slams. The victim drops.*
> *The ONLOOKERS cheer. SARAH's*
> *knees give way, but MACDONALD*
> *catches her before she hits the ground.*

MACDONALD   It's not your father, Miss Chandler. (*beat*) At
least, not yet.

> *MARIA rushes on carrying her a baby and*
> *also a worn carpet bag. A man's large gold*
> *pocket watch is pinned prominently on her*
> *dress.*

MARIA	(*to ONLOOKERS*) Who is it?
ONLOOKER 1	A murdering rebel!
MARIA	His name? (*appealing to ANNIE*) Tell me his name?
ANNIE	(*shaking her head*) He's some American.
ONLOOKER 2	Yankee scum.
MARIA	(*greatly relieved*) God rest his soul.
ANNIE	(*warning*) Hold your whist.
ONLOOKER 2	(*overlapping*) Damn him to hell, you mean!
MARIA	(*to ONLOOKER*) He's dying for your freedom!
ONLOOKER 1	Hey! She's a rebel lover!

The ONLOOKERS close in on MARIA. She begins to sing defiantly:

MARIA

Up and waur'em all, Willie
Up and waur'em all
Better brave the tyrant's frown
Than see your country fall.

After the first line of MARIA's song, everyone starts yelling at once.

ONLOOKER 2	(*overlapping ANNIE*) Shut up, bitch.
MACDONALD	(*pulling SARAH away*) Watch out...quick...
ONLOOKER 1	Grab her!
ANNIE	(*to Maria*) Get out of here! Run!
ONLOOKER 2	(*overlapping ANNIE while trying to grab MARIA*) Let's hang her too!

*WHEELER and the GUARD head off the
ONLOOKERS. MARIA runs off.*

MACDONALD   (*looking after MARIA*) That woman must be
mad.

SARAH   (*having scarcely noticed the fight*) Mr.
MacDonald, did you say 'Not yet'?

MACDONALD   (*taking a list from his pocket*) Your father's
being held in that jail. Charged with the same
treason for which (*pointing to the dangling
victim*) this unfortunate was condemned.

SARAH   That's impossible!

MACDONALD   (*passing the list to her*) See for yourself.
(*pointing out a name*) Samuel Chandler, land
owner. Married, seven children. (*as SARAH
stares at it in disbelief*) Miss Chandler, you must
have known he'd joined the rebels?

SARAH   No...

MACDONALD   Then where did you think he was?

SARAH   Nowhere...I mean...A man came to the door...and
he just disappeared .

MACDONALD   Without explanation?

SARAH   But he can't be a traitor...not my Papa!

*The ONLOOKERS react as WHEELER
and the HANGMAN cut the victim down.*

ONLOOKER 1   Ain't you supposed to quarter him up?

ONLOOKER 2   Wasn't worth the trip to town.

*SARAH starts off in the direction of the
jail. MACDONALD grabs her arm.*

SARAH   I want to see him!

MACDONALD   You can't go in until the execution's over! Remember, I tried to delay you.

SARAH   (*pausing and gaining control of herself*) Mr. MacDonald, have you talked to him?

MACDONALD   That's why I asked your mother to come here...I have no access until a prisoner, or a member of his family, requests my assistance.

SARAH   (*giving him back the list*) Then...you're only assuming he's guilty? You have no proof?

> *HANGMAN and GUARD carry the body off.*

MACDONALD   Samuel Chandler was captured on the field of battle, wearing that uniform. (*indicating the uniform on the body*) The uniform of the so-called Patriot army.

> *SARAH stares after the men who exit with the body*

His trial begins on Thursday, and without legal representation, by this time next week, it will be your Papa those men are carrying off to be quartered.

SARAH   (*beat*) Were you that man's lawyer?

MACDONALD   No, I wasn't. (*half a beat*) No client of mine has ever been executed.

SARAH   (*looking at him with new eyes*) Oh.

MACDONALD   (*struck by her gaze*) Believe me, my dear, all I'm asking is the chance to help you?

SARAH   All right...yes, help me, please.

> *The HANGMAN and WHEELER return. WHEELER is counting coins into the HANGMAN'S hand.*

ONLOOKER 2   (*blocking HANGMAN's path*) How much you
              get?

ONLOOKER 3   What's the colour of blood money, Ketch?

              *The HANGMAN tries to exit, backing
              into LIZZIE who recoils in terror.*

ANNIE   (*reassuring her*) There, there. He's just a wretch
              with mouths to feed.

WHEELER   Get on to your homes, if you got any. Nothing
              more to gawk at here.

              *ONLOOKERS disperse. LIZZIE and
              ANNIE linger, watching SARAH.*

MACDONALD   (*to WHEELER*) My client wishes admission to
              the cells.

WHEELER   My list was worth the price, eh? You finally got
              your first case!

              *SARAH looks at MACDONALD in
              dismay.*

MACDONALD   Mr. Wheeler, this is no time for jokes.

WHEELER   All right. Show me your pass.

MACDONALD   Unless the law's changed overnight, blood
              relatives don't need a pass.

WHEELER   I got new orders from Toronto this morning.
              (*whispering*) It was a Yankee hung, see.
              Government's scared of reprisals.

MACDONALD   (*laughing*) Come, man, you can't take this young
              lady for an American invasion?

WHEELER   She could be a spy, since she's kin to a rebel.

SARAH   But I'm not. I'm certain there's been a mistake.

WHEELER	(*reassessing her and changing his tone*) Sorry, miss. I'm just doing my job.
SARAH	May I at least send in a note?
WHEELER	There's no communication at all. Not without the Justice's say so.

WHEELER exits.

SARAH	(*to MACDONALD*) The Justice..?
MACDONALD	The Chief Justice. I'll have to forward a request to his office.
SARAH	How long will that take?
MACDONALD	I could dispatch a messenger by the Toronto ferry boat. If you wish to stand the expense?
SARAH	(*opening her purse and taking out some large coins*) Never mind the cost.
MACDONALD	(*taking one and closing SARAH's hand on the rest*) Have a care...there are thieves about.

ANNIE sees the coins and quickly moves in. LIZZIE follows her.

ANNIE	Miss, excuse me, miss.
MACDONALD	This is a private conversation.
ANNIE	(*to MACDONALD*) I couldn't help overhearing it. (*to SARAH*) And from what I heard, you'll be needing a boarding house here in town.
MACDONALD	(*seeing SARAH's hesitation*) Surely you should go and fetch your mother?
SARAH	(*upset*) She's convinced Papa's dead...she'd be hysterical...
MACDONALD	Miss Chandler, you can't stay here on your own.

ANNIE   Sure, you'll come to no harm at Annie Beemer's.
                 Isn't my son in the cell right next to your Pa?

MACDONALD   Oh?

SARAH   Thank you. I'll take the room.

MACDONALD   Well, if you're determined .

SARAH   I am, Mr. MacDonald. I'm not leaving Niagara
                 till I find out the truth.

MACDONALD   I was going to say...the famous falls aren't far
                 from town. Perhaps, later...you might like to
                 ride out to them?

SARAH   I don't need another spectacle, thank you. I need
                 to be alone.

MACDONALD   (*crushed*) Of course. Can you make your way to
                 my office in the morning?

                 LIZZIE tugs on SARAH's hand.

ANNIE   (*to MACDONALD*) I'll see she gets there.

LIZZIE   (*exiting with SARAH*) It's a new house. We just
                 buy'd it.

                 ANNIE is about to follow.

MACDONALD   Mrs. Beemer...I surmise your son is a rebel?

ANNIE   (*turning back*) Some say a rebel, some say a
                 patriot. There's those say a fool.

MACDONALD   Even a fool is entitled to legal advice.

ANNIE   Even a fool with no money, sir?

MACDONALD   You own a boarding house. Something could be
                 arranged.

ANNIE	I already lost the tavern, I'll not lose my house in the bargain.
MACDONALD	(*eagerly*) Did the Crown confiscate property before your son's trial?
ANNIE	The tavern was burned, along with every stick I was owned of.
MACDONALD	Then how did you manage to buy a new house?
ANNIE	Oh, the devil looks after his own. And from what I've seen of lawyers, sir, that should be as much comfort to you as to me.

> *ANNIE exits in one direction.*
> *MACDONALD looks after her a moment,*
> *then exits in the other, as this scene*
> *segues right into the next scene...*

Scene Two

A ROOM IN ANNIE'S BOARDING HOUSE

> *...SARAH enters, carrying a small,*
> *store-wrapped parcel. LIZZIE drags on a*
> *cot.*

SARAH	Papa a rebel! He never even bothered to vote! Oh, Lizzie, I'm so upset...(*looking around for a place to put her parcel, then laying it on the floor*) I don't know if I'm coming or going.
LIZZIE	I don't know my arse from my elbow.
SARAH	No, dear, no. You mustn't use vulgarities...no matter what happens, young ladies remember who they are. (*taking off her bonnet and scarf*)

SARAH   (*continued*) We don't give silly tears a chance.We get on with the tasks at hand. (*passing the bonnet and scarf to LIZZIE who lays them on the bed*) The first thing is a note to mother...

> *ANNIE enters with a blanket and sheet, as SARAH picks up her parcel and pauses, stuck for an idea.*

Mrs. Beemer, if I say I didn't find Papa, what excuse can I give for staying overnight?

ANNIE   Twist your ankle, miss. (*putting the bonnet and scarf on the floor as she makes up the bed, sloppily*) Then you can break it should the need arise.

SARAH   I'll go home tomorrow...as long as Mr. MacDonald secures my pass.After what the jailer said, I'm not sure I can rely on him...

ANNIE   Rely on, is it? Lizzie, tell the lady where you find somebody you can rely on?

LIZZIE   (*shyly*) In your own looking glass.

> *A knock or a bell is heard. LIZZIE exits.*

SARAH   (*dismissive*) No, no. I need to think of someone important...(*racking her brains*) There's the Colonel...I suppose he might know the Chief Justice...(*an idea explodes in her mind*) Oh, oh, Mrs. Beemer! Is John Beverley Robinson still the Chief Justice?

ANNIE   (*ironic*) As he was in the beginning, is now and ever shall be, amen.

SARAH   (*breathless with excitement*) What time is the ferry to Toronto?

ANNIE   The next one's at three.

SARAH   (*heading to her parcel*) I've just remembered someone I can write to! Someone whose single word might make them set Papa free!

ANNIE   (*alert*) You think he could spare a syllable for my Jake?

SARAH   Well...(*looking for a way out*) I'm not certain he'll even remember me. We only shared a dance at the Coronation Ball.

ANNIE   Then you got to get him to see you. You want to be able to wiggle your figure.

SARAH   (*shocked*) The acquaintance I refer to is a gentleman.

ANNIE   Miss, neither prince nor pauper is going to turn down what you have to offer.

SARAH   Any man of honour would be disgusted by your suggestion. As, I might add, am I.

> *SARAH turns her back on ANNIE and unwraps her parcel of writing materials as LIZZIE enters and whispers to ANNIE.*

ANNIE   (*to SARAH*) Take a hint from me, miss...you'd best give over those airs and graces of yours. (*moving to exit*) They'll bring you nothing but grief now you can't afford them.

SARAH   Just a moment!

> *ANNIE turns back.*

You are bringing more furniture?

ANNIE   What more do you want?

SARAH   I need a table and chair.

ANNIE   (*moving again*) There's a table and chair in the kitchen.

SARAH	Mrs. Beemer...
ANNIE	(*quickly*) I've a poor house, I'll grant you. But grander places aren't keen on the daughters of jailbirds.

> *As ANNIE exits, SARAH turns to see LIZZIE trying on her scarf.*

SARAH	No! (*taking the scarf from LIZZIE*) No, Lizzie, this is very precious.
LIZZIE	It's pretty.
SARAH	(*holding it close to her*) Papa imported the lace for me, all the way from Belgium.
LIZZIE	Bel...jum. That's where my Da is.
SARAH	(*off hand*) I think you mean Belfast.

> *SARAH lays sheet of paper on the bed and kneels on the floor.*

LIZZIE	(*shaking her head*) He's dead.
SARAH	I'm sorry....(*noticing dirt on the floor and jumping up*) Oh, heavens! (*checking the hem of her skirt, and attempting to wipe the floor with her sleeve*) Oh, no dear, no. Even your mother must have someone to clean for her? (*LIZZIE nods*) Then you go fetch her to me. (*LIZZIE looks blank, since she is that person, and doesn't move*) Run along, Lizzie.

> *LIZZIE exits. SARAH takes a pillow from the bed and kneels on that. She opens the bottle of ink and takes up her pen. As she begins her letter, MARIA WAIT enters, carrying the baby. She is humming "Up and Waur'em all Willie" as if it were a lullaby.*

MARIA	(*to the audience*) God is definitely on the side of Reform. (*to the baby*) He must be, pet. He brought us to this house so we can bring cheer to Dada. (*beat*) You don't care, do you? You don't even know who Dada is. Well, you're going to know! There'll be a next time, and next time we're going to win. You'll grow up in a free country, where all the people have a say in what goes on. Upper Canada will have a parliament responsible to the people, even if Mama has to take up a gun and shoot all the Tories herself! (*to the audience*) If only I could have fought the last time.If only my baby had picked a better time to be born. (*turning into the room and speaking to SARAH*) Miss Chandler?
SARAH	(*looking up*) That was quick. Where's your mop and pail?
MARIA	I beg your pardon?
SARAH	Aren't you the scrub woman?
MARIA	(*moving right in and sitting on the cot*) Lord, no. I'm Maria Wait. And I'm desperate to get in touch with my husband.
SARAH	(*snatching her scarf out of the way*) I assure you, ma'am, you won't find him in my bedroom.
MARIA	(*laughing*) Oh, I know that. I just spent my last shilling for a nod from the jailer.
SARAH	You're the woman who started the riot.
MARIA	(*delighted*) And you're the answer to my prayers! Isn't it marvelous we're sharing a room?
SARAH	What? No, you've made a mistake.
	ANNIE enters. LIZZIE follows with a second pillow.
ANNIE	You two getting acquainted, all right?

SARAH	Mrs. Beemer, (*taking ANNIE aside as LIZZIE picks up the baby*) I paid to have private accommodation.
ANNIE	Sure I only have the kitchen besides, and isn't her man in the cell right next to your pa?
SARAH	(*to ANNIE*) I thought your son was in that cell!
ANNIE	There's two sides to everything, miss. Your pa's in the middle.
MARIA	(*going to SARAH*) That's why you're in a perfect position to help me.
ANNIE	(*to MARIA*) One thing at a time, girl. (*pushing LIZZIE with the baby closer to SARAH*) Miss, you're not going to begrudge a Christian and her mite a place to lie their heads?
MARIA	(*incredulous*) Of course she's not!
LIZZIE	(*sing song*) Pretty baby mite.
SARAH	(*looking at the baby and giving in*) Oh...
LIZZIE	...don't know if she's coming or going.
SARAH	...if there's no other choice. (*crossing to continue her letter*)
ANNIE	(*immediately, to MARIA*) So, Mrs. Wait, you said you could pay in kind?
MARIA	(*taking an old pair of boots from her bag and passing them to ANNIE, but her attention is still on SARAH*) Miss Chandler, all I need you to do is whisper some hope to my husband.
SARAH	(*writing*) Mrs. Wait, I'm busy at the moment.
ANNIE	(*rejecting the boots*) A bit worn, ain't they?

MARIA	(*to SARAH*) I mean tomorrow, when you get your pass...
SARAH	(*looking up*) Who told you —
ANNIE	(*quickly*) Now you two have the whole evening to natter...(*to MARIA*) What about that time-piece on your dress?

> *SARAH goes back to her letter. LIZZIE settles the baby on the pillow.*

MARIA	(*touching it*) This was my father's.
ANNIE	I could haggle a price for real gold.
MARIA	(*more a plea than a refusal*) I couldn't...it was all he had to leave me.
ANNIE	Girl, I'd love to board you for nothing, if I hadn't spent my last ha-pence taking food to that jail.
MARIA	Oh...(*unpinning the watch*) bless you.
ANNIE	Without one word of a lie, all thirty of them would have starved if it wasn't for me.
MARIA	Then you've seen Ben?
SARAH	(*looking up, eagerly*) Have you seen my father?
ANNIE	Every day till this one.
MARIA	(*giving her the watch*) He isn't in despair, is he?
SARAH	(*rushing to ANNIE*) Did Papa say anything?
ANNIE	They're both alive and standing.
SARAH	That there'd been a mistake?
ANNIE	Well...(*pausing*)
LIZZIE	Jailer won't let us talk to more than our Jake.

ANNIE   (*meaning 'be quiet'*) Lizzie...

MARIA   He won't? (*to ANNIE*) You told me Miss
               Chandler could take Ben a message?

ANNIE   Sure, didn't I forget about the jailer. Well, you're
               no worse off than you were, girl, and at least
               you've got a bed to rest your bones.

SARAH   You don't expect me to share my bed!

ANNIE   Why not? Your men put you in the same one
               anyways.

MARIA   (*to SARAH*) Never mind...the floor will do me.

SARAH   The floor isn't fit to walk on, let alone sleep on.

ANNIE   (*to SARAH*) I'd say a bit of dust is the least of
               her worries...even if it seems to be the most of
               yours. Come on, Lizzie, (*exiting*) time to peel
               the spuds.

LIZZIE   (*leaving the baby reluctantly*) We gotta get on
               with the tasks at hand. (*exiting*)

SARAH   (*resuming her letter*) Yes, we do.

MARIA   (*looking over at SARAH and forming an idea*)
               That's it! That's the remedy! (*as SARAH looks at
               her*) Please, might I borrow some of that paper?

SARAH   The shop is right next door.

MARIA   A sheet would do. Even a half sheet. (*SARAH
               passes it*) And are you finished with the pen?

SARAH   No, I'm not.

MARIA   I'll wait then. (*positioning herself on the floor to
               write*) That's irony for you...Maria Wait...when
               nobody hates waiting more than me. (*with a
               touch of pride*) I was born Maria Randal.

> *MARIA expects a reaction but SARAH
> folds her letter without any response.
> MARIA reaches over for the pen.*

SARAH   (*ironic*) You're welcome.

MARIA   (*oblivious*) May I have the ink too? (*as SARAH
looks at her*) Well, the one's not much good
without the other.

> *SARAH passes it, then dresses to go out
> as MARIA begins her letter.*

Oh, this is much better. I can be more...personal
...and you can simply drop it in Ben's cell.

SARAH   May I suggest you simply get a pass of your
own?

MARIA   (*as if the connection were obvious*) I told
you...I'm a Randal.

SARAH   Am I supposed to recognize that name?

MARIA   My father was Robert Randal. (*seeing her
ignorance*) The founder of the Reform party?
(*still no response*) The first arch-enemy of our
Chief *In*-Justice?

SARAH   (*instinctively hiding her letter*) I'm afraid I've
never been interested in (*it's a dirty word*)
politics. (*moving toward the exit*) I regret I can't
be of assistance.

MARIA   (*after her*) But you have to! Your father would
expect you to!

SARAH   (*rounding on her*) What do you know of my
father?

MARIA   He didn't tell William Lyon Mackenzie he
"couldn't be of assistance"!

SARAH   Papa had nothing to do with Mackenzie!

MARIA	(*taken aback*) Mac was a stranger who knocked at your door. The same way I knocked on this one.
SARAH	(*suspicious*) When?
MARIA	When he had to flee the country.Don't you know the story?
SARAH	(*light dawning*) Was Mackenzie a small man with stringy red hair?
MARIA	He still is! Because your father took out his boat and rowed him across the river to The States.
SARAH	(*excited*) Mrs. Wait, come quickly...
MARIA	Why? What for?
SARAH	You can prove Papa is innocent! That all he did was an act of charity!
MARIA	To begin with...but he's been fighting along side my husband ever since.
SARAH	No...
MARIA	He became a true patriot. That's why he'd want you to help me.
SARAH	I don't believe you...You're lying to me... (*breaking down*) Everybody's lying ...
MARIA	(*going to her*) What's wrong?
SARAH	(*over MARIA's line*) It's all lies!
MARIA	You should be proud of him!
SARAH	Proud! Proud that he's going to hang!
MARIA	Don't say that! Miss Chandler, despair is our worst enemy. I've come here to make sure my Ben fights tooth and nail for his life. You must do the same for your father.

SARAH   Leave me alone.

MARIA   Listen to me...They need to believe they have a
             chance, and they do. The jury will be different.
             The outcome could be too. And even if it
             isn't...Listen, I was going to trust you with this
             anyway, I went to The States to have Augusta,
             and I heard there's ten thousand men marshalled
             there now...all ready and waiting for the chance
             to march!

SARAH   (*incredulous*) Ten thousand rebels?

MARIA   Ten thousand patriots! And you know what I
             think...I think that hanging today is going to do
             them some good. You see, up till now the
             President's been afraid to give them arms, but
             once they hear John Robinson has killed a
             Yankee, all the Americans will be chomping at
             the bit.

SARAH   I don't care about Americans.

MARIA   But they're going to come and set us free! Not
             only my husband and your father! The whole
             country! (*indicating letter*) That's the message I
             want to get to Ben, see.

SARAH   That's what you've been writing on my paper?
             (*attempting to wrest the paper and ink bottle
             from MARIA who holds on*) Give it back!

MARIA   What's the matter?

SARAH   You are lying about my father! And I know why!
             Because you're a rebel yourself!

MARIA   Of course I am!

             Ink spatters on SARAH's scarf.

SARAH   (*breaking from the fight*) Oh, you horrible,
             horrible woman! I will never do anything to help
             you! Never!

> *SARAH runs off. MARIA goes to the baby and picks her up.*

MARIA
"Up and waur'em all", Augusta. Let's see if Mrs. Beemer has some ink. Oh pet, when will your mama learn to save her breath. At least around empty headed ninnies like —

> *MARIA exits as...*

Scene Three

THE GARDEN OF BEVERLEY HOUSE, TORONTO

> *...EMMA ROBINSON, an elegant matron, enters carrying an unopened letter.*

EMMA
(*as if continuing MARIA's line*)...Miss S. Chandler?

> *Lights change to indicate a garden in early evening. A SERVANT follows with a garden chair, as others remove the cot.*

SERVANT
Delivered up from the ferryboat, Missus Justus.

EMMA
(*correcting him*) Mrs. Robinson.

SERVANT
(*glancing up as EMMA considers opening the letter*) It's addressed to Master Lukin.

EMMA
(*lowering the letter and pointing*) Over here, please, out of the sun.

SERVANT
Hardly worth the effort, missus. Sun's about set.

EMMA
Patrick, do as I ask.

The SERVANT reluctantly moves the chair and exits, as EMMA addresses the audience. She is bristling with repressed anger.

My husband assures me that the rebellion was a tempest in a teapot. Well, (*referring to the SERVANT*) the leaves left in my cup predict a dire fortune. Oh, our servants would never express overt sympathy for Reformers, but they no longer bother with a semblance of respect. John says I need a firmer hand. I say John's whistling in the dark. It's true the Reformers failed to throw him out of office, but they have made a mockery of the preeminence we hoped to achieve, both for Toronto and Upper Canada. It's because of their rebellion, that the British Government has sent out the Earl of Durham, first cousin of Victoria herself, to be Royal Commissioner for all of British North America...

DURHAM enters. He is a youthful forty, and, like Lord Byron, a Romantic aristocrat of feverish extremes who provokes either deep love or deep hatred. Although he knows he has consumption, he absolutely refuses to give into illness or self pity. Instead he is driven to make his final task a noble one.

DURHAM   I shall stamp the seal of justice on this new land.

EMMA   His report will determine our future...our children's future as well...

DURHAM   The Durham Report will set the settlers of Canada free!

EMMA   Yet London chose not to send him to us in Toronto. (*the ultimate outrage*) They have sent him to be governor of Quebec.

DURHAM   (*with a paper, puzzled*) According to this brief, Quebec is the capital of *Lower* Canada...(*reading further*) Oh, there's an Upper one! Don't tell me it has a governor too!

EMMA   And, to add insult to injury, London has afflicted us with a complete nonentity...

DURHAM   Sir George Arthur?

SIR GEORGE ARTHUR, Governor of Upper Canada. ARTHUR is of an earlier generation, rigid and uncompromising. He is a middle-class Englishman who rose to the position of ruler through the ranks of military and civil service.

ARTHUR   (*to the audience*) I may not be Durham's equal in rank, but I am his equal in office. Why is he asked for a report and not I?

ARTHUR and DURHAM freeze.

EMMA   (*intimately*) I wouldn't want the servants to hear this, but in his former colony, our governor had a nickname....

SERVANT   Oh, missus..

EMMA   Yes, Patrick?

SERVANT   Cook wants to know will the Justus have et with "The Butcher"?

EMMA   (*putting her hand over her face in despair*) Oh, no.

SERVANT   (*taking this for a answer*) You heard, eh? He hanged four hundred men in his last place.

EMMA   (*to the audience*) Of course, it was a penal colony. They *were* convicts.

> *LUKIN ROBINSON enters. He's in his early twenties, very fashionable. He's carrying a magazine.* The Albion.

LUKIN   (*offering the magazine*) Present for you, mumsy.

EMMA   (*ignoring the magazine and thrusting SARAH's letter at him*) Lukin, who is Miss S. Chandler?

LUKIN   I've no idea.

EMMA   Perhaps someone you succeeded in sneaking up my stairs?

LUKIN   Mother, there was only one girl.

EMMA   One your father caught you with.

LUKIN   Cross my heart, I don't know any Miss Chandler.

EMMA   Then why is she writing to you?

LUKIN   Open it and see. (*looking as if she will*) If you refuse to trust my word of honour.

> *EMMA backs down and holds it out to LUKIN. He takes it with his left hand and offers her the magazine from his right.*

    (*teasing*) Now I've something to take your frown away.

EMMA   (*curious, but reluctant to give in*) I've no interest in scandal.

LUKIN   Even when...My little mumsy is not going to be displaced as first lady of Upper Canada?

EMMA   Oh?

LUKIN   (*pointing out an article*) Arthur's wife was so devastated that he was appointed here instead of to India that she's refusing to leave England.

EMMA   (*with a poor attempt at concealing her pleasure*)
                 As if a mere baronet could get India.

                 *JOHN BEVERLEY ROBINSON, Chief
                 Justice of Upper Canada, a fine looking
                 man in his late forties, enters. He's not in
                 a good mood.*

LUKIN   Father, (*quickly pocketing the letter*) you're
                 early...

ROBINSON   Ah, Lukin, good. Emma, I have bad news.

EMMA   (*dropping the magazine on her chair*) There's been
                 another uprising!

ROBINSON   No, no. I've some business out of town, that's
                 all. Could you order our bags to be packed?

LUKIN   Our? Do you mean mine?

EMMA   (*before he can answer*) John, you have a fitting
                 tonight.

ROBINSON   I'm sorry, my dear...

EMMA   If your costume's not ready, my ball will be
                 ruined.

ROBINSON   We must be settled in and at work by morning.
                 Please, Emma, do as I ask.

                 EMMA exits.

LUKIN   (*moving to him*) Sir, I've made plans for this
                 evening.

ROBINSON   Lukin...I don't want your mother to hear a word
                 of this. That fool George Arthur is trying to ruin
                 me.

ARTHUR   (*from his position*) I've no intention of allowing
                 the Durham Report to put the blame on me!

LUKIN   (*offhand*) New governors are always sticky,
               father. You'll bring him round.

ROBINSON   This is serious...look what I found in the
               government files. (*passing an official letter to
               LUKIN*)

                    *DURHAM takes an identical document
                    from his pocket and reads silently.*

LUKIN   (*sitting and reading aloud*) " To the Earl of
               Durham..?

ROBINSON   Thank God the clerk made a copy...

LUKIN   (*in unison with ARTHUR*) Regarding the
               continuing violence in my colony..."

ARTHUR   (*in unison*)...the continuing violence in my
               colony..."

LUKIN   (*looking up*) We haven't had much violence
               lately.

ROBINSON   Read it...read what mountains can be made of
               molehills!

                    LUKIN reads the letter silently.

ARTHUR   I've discovered that the Executive Counsellor I
               inherited, a colonial called...John Robinson..

DURHAM   (*in unison with ARTHUR*)...John Robinson...

ARTHUR   (*continuing alone*) ..is himself the focus of
               widespread discontent, (*as LUKIN emits a sharp
               whistle*) and that for reasons of self-interest, he
               persuaded my predecessor to underestimate the
               threat to British rule. I enclose, as proof of the
               chaos I must contend with, a request from the
               Upper Canadian Militia for increased munitions
               and supplies. Your lordship may read for himself
               the account of their most recent battle,

LUKIN	What battle?
ROBINSON	(*impatient*) That piddling raid from across the border...
ARTHUR	Wherein, aided only by the Grace of God, five hundred militiamen triumphed over a rebel force which outnumbered them three to one.
LUKIN	(*in unison*) "...a rebel force which outnumbered them three to one."
DURHAM	(*after them*) "...a rebel force which outnumbered them three to one! "

ARTHUR exits.

LUKIN	This must be a joke.
DURHAM	(*joyful*) Fifteen hundred voices ...crying out for me!
ROBINSON	That letter was dispatched two weeks ago. I found out about it today because (*picking up the magazine*) *The Albion* got wind of Durham's reply.
LUKIN	Oh...I didn't get that far.
ROBINSON	(*tossing him the magazine*) Her Majesty's High Commissioner is not content with *reading* for himself....
DURHAM	(*running off*) Procure me a ship!
ROBINSON	He's decided to come and *hear* for himself.
LUKIN	(*glancing at the headline*) Oh, father, he's coming to see the Falls.
ROBINSON	Smack in the middle of the rebel trials? Don't you believe it. (*calling off*) Emma, how long can it take to pack a few clothes!

LUKIN   I don't understand why we're rushing off. All that
               will happen is he'll learn the truth.

ROBINSON   He's known as Radical Jack, for God's sake.
               (*indicating the magazine*) It's all in there...(*as
               LUKIN reads silently*) In our noble Queen's
               cousin beats a vile and democratic heart. If he
               believes a single word of what one rebel is likely
               to drag up against me, that Report of his will do
               more harm than the rebellion ever did. I can't risk
               it, my boy, I have to prevent the rebels from
               testifying.

LUKIN   (*putting* The Albion *down*) Too bad you stopped
               the militia from shooting them on the spot.

ROBINSON   Preserving the rule of law is the point, for God's
               sake! (*lecturing*) The rule of law is the foundation
               on which I've built this colony. The foundation
               on which you will build this nation!

LUKIN   Yes, sir.

ROBINSON   There are legal ways to keep them quiet. I've had
               a note from a rebel lawyer who may be of
               use...(*stopping as EMMA enters*)

EMMA   Patrick's put your bags in the carriage, but surely
               you have time to eat.

ROBINSON   (*shaking his head*) The Government boat is
               standing by. (*moving*) Lukin...

EMMA   A boat? Where is it you're going?

ROBINSON   Niagara. Will you come and see us off?

                    *ROBINSON pauses to let EMMA precede
                    him off.*

LUKIN   Father! I have an idea already.

ROBINSON   Yes?

LUKIN	Couldn't you simply postpone the trials?
ROBINSON	Yes, I could, Lukin. I could also hire a town crier to announce I have something to hide.

> *They exit. The SERVANT enters to remove furniture.*

EMMA	(*running on*) Patrick, Lukin's letter...delivered from the ferry boat.
SERVANT	Yes, missus?
EMMA	Which ferryboat?
SERVANT	The one from Niagara, missus.
EMMA	Damn.

> *EMMA exits and...*

Scene Four

THE JAIL AT NIAGARA

> *...lights change to indicate early morning. MARIA enters, carrying the baby.*

MARIA	(*singing to the baby, while "casing the joint"*) "Up and waur 'em, Willie...Up at the crack of dawn." Augusta, we're so close we could reach Dada through a window. If the jail had a window.

> *WHEELER and LUKIN enter. MARIA shrinks back.*

WHEELER	(*shaking his head*) Yesterday he wants nobody in. Today I'm supposed to hold a picnic for half the colony!
LUKIN	(*with a card*) Where might I find this office?
WHEELER	(*pointing*) Around the corner, sir.

> *LUKIN exits. WHEELER notices MARIA.*

What are you doing there?

MARIA	I'm looking for a way to break in to my husband. If you want to help by arresting me, please do.
WHEELER	No need to fuss. Justice changed his mind again.
MARIA	I can see Ben?
WHEELER	Ben Wait? I'll fetch him to the yard. But no whispering, (*exiting*) or he's back in the cell.
MARIA	(*to the baby, as she slips a letter in under the baby's clothes*) I know it's uncomfortable, pet, but think of all Dada's suffered for us.

> *WHEELER shoves BEN WAIT into the yard. He's about Maria's age, attractive, wearing a ragged Patriot jacket. He has chains on his hands and feet. He has no idea why he's out of his cell.*

MARIA	(*with a pretense of lightness*) Look at you!
BEN	Maria!

> *BEN turns away in shame and confusion.*

MARIA	(*moving towards him*) Safe and sound with a roof over your head...
WHEELER	(*over her line*) No touching neither!

MARIA   All the time I was out searching ditches for your
               body!

BEN   (*with conflicting emotions*) You promised you'd
               stay in Buffalo.

MARIA   I wanted to, Ben. (*holding the baby toward him*)
               See who couldn't sit still until she found her
               dada?

WHEELER   (*warning*) None of that!

BEN   (*not able to look at the baby*) Have you no sense
               at all! You should have left her at your brother's.

MARIA   My brother doesn't have what this child needs
               every few hours. I hate to tell you, Ben, our
               Augusta's as greedy as any Toronto Tory.

BEN   (*hearing the name for the first time*) Augusta...

MARIA   I thought of Benjamina, but it seemed an awful
               thing to do to a poor innocent. Besides, we'll
               probably have a boy next time.

BEN   (*trying to stop her*) Maria...

MARIA   (*quickly*) We can start him right after your trial.
               Maybe before they take your chains off...

BEN   Stop it! Please stop! The best comfort you can
               give me is to go straight to The States.

MARIA   I'm not leaving you, and I'm not leaving my
               country!

BEN   The country is finished, and so am I!

MARIA   Hush your nonsense! Take your baby.

WHEELER   (*moving on her*) I warned you —

MARIA   (*rounding on him*) How could it hurt your Tory
               bosses to let a man hold his own child!

> *MACDONALD and SARAH enter. He carries a writing box with pen, ink and documents.*

MACDONALD   (*with new found authority*) Mr. Wheeler!

> *WHEELER crosses to MACDONALD. SARAH watches BEN and MARIA.*

MARIA   Come on, take her! (*thrusting the baby into his arms*) That's it.

BEN   (*looking at his child for the first time*) I thought I'd never see her.

MARIA   Cradle her head.

BEN   Oh, Maria...she's beautiful.

MARIA   (*whispering*) Now reach into her nappie.

BEN   What?

WHEELER   (*crossing upstage and calling to a guard off*) Send out Sam Chandler.

MARIA   Quick! You'll find more than you might expect.

> *As the astonished BEN finds the letter and pockets it, MARIA angles herself to be between BEN and WHEELER. She notices SARAH watching them.*

(*to SARAH*) Stop staring! (*for WHEELER's benefit*) See, Ben. The poor pet's got your ears.

> *SAM appears, wearing the same jacket as BEN. BEN and MARIA draw aside.*

MACDONALD   (*to SARAH*) I'll give you a few moments.

> *SAM rushes to SARAH. MACDONALD opens his box and takes out papers.*

SAM   You found me!

WHEELER   No touching!

SARAH   (*shrinking back from his uniform*) It's all true...

SAM   What's wrong? The uniform? It's still your old
                 Papa inside. (*as SARAH draws away from him*)
                 Your mother and your sisters, are they all right?

SARAH   They think you were trapped in a fire.

SAM   You mean Comfort's place? (*as SARAH nods*)
                 Didn't you get any of the messages I sent? (*as
                 SARAH shakes her head*) Oh, lass...I tried a
                 dozen different ways.

                         ANNIE enters.

WHEELER   (*calling as he sees ANNIE*) Fetch Jake Beemer.

MACDONALD   Excuse me, you'll have plenty of time for
                 explanations.

SARAH   (*making an effort*) Papa, my lawyer, Mr.
                 MacDonald, has some news.

MACDONALD   And not just for you, sir. (*public address*) Would
                 you all step over here please?

                         *ALL go to him except WHEELER who
                         sits and watches from a distance. JAKE
                         appears.*

JAKE   What's this then?

MACDONALD   You prisoners know that you're charged with
                 murder, theft and treason.

SAM   No one was killed, young man.

JAKE   Nothing was stolen neither.

MACDONALD	A Martin Overholt swears he was robbed of one thousand dollars.
ANNIE & JAKE	(*in unison*) Why that lying sleeveen!
MACDONALD	Well...the matter no longer signifies. A few moments ago, a communication from the Crown arrived at my office. (*magnanimously*) You are to be prosecuted only for treason.
JAKE	Do it matter what we hang for?
BEN	Jake, let him speak.
MACDONALD	And on that charge, the Crown will ask for no more than a brief term in prison!

The reactions overlap.

ANNIE	(*joyous*) Holy Mother of God!
SAM	(*to SARAH*) Is it true?
MARIA	(*joyous*) Ben —
BEN	Hold on! (*to MACDONALD*) What are the conditions?
MACDONALD	You are merely required to confess that you were misled into rash and unprovoked rebellion —
MARIA	Unprovoked!
MACDONALD	— by the lies and false promises of unprincipled American agitators.
MARIA	You're asking them to betray everything they fought for!
MACDONALD	Madam, the Chief Justice is offering them a way to save their lives. (*passing out papers*) Mr. Chandler...

SARAH	(*taking the pen and holding it to SAM*) Sign it, Papa. Then I can go tell Mamma you're safe.
SAM	Give me time to read it, lassie.
MACDONALD	I'm afraid there's some legal terminology.
BEN	I can manage, sir. I've studied law.
ANNIE	(*grabbing the pen from SARAH*) Jake'll put his X.
JAKE	Aye, give it here.
	SAM and BEN study the documents. JAKE takes the pen from ANNIE and makes his X.
MARIA	(*about to argue*) Mrs. Beemer.
BEN	(*restraining her*) Jake's case is different. Let's deal with our own.
ANNIE	(*hugging JAKE*) What a load off, eh!
WHEELER	(*separating them*) That's it! (*giving JAKE a shove toward the jail*) Go on! (*to MACDONALD*) You want the rest, you go inside yourself.
ANNIE	(*to MARIA*) Girl, I'll see you back at the house.
MACDONALD	(*hearing the word "house" he gets an idea*) Jake! (*catching up with JAKE and exiting with him*) About your mother's house..
ANNIE	(*an afterthought*) You want I should take the mite with me?
BEN	Yes, Maria. There's fever here.
	The baby is transferred to ANNIE who exits with her.
SAM	Ben, what's the profit for Robinson in this rubbish?

BEN	Signing it is the same as pleading guilty. He saves himself the trouble of giving us trial.
MARIA	(*whispering*) He must think he'd lose...
WHEELER	No whispering!
SARAH	You were here yesterday, you saw a man hanged!
MARIA	(*impatient*) I told you! He was an American!
SARAH	(*louder*) What difference does it make!
WHEELER	No shouting neither!
BEN	Miss Chandler, it's possible a jury had no sympathy for a foreign invader. As Canadians, we could argue we were driven to rebellion...
SARAH	But...
SAM	Quiet, lass...(*to BEN*) Say, by some miracle, they refused to convict us, might that be embarrassing for Robinson?
BEN	An acquittal for us would be a condemnation of the government, but —
MARIA	Then that's what he's afraid of!
BEN	(*continuing firmly*) But it would be a miracle.
MARIA	You had no choice, and we can prove it. I'll find the documents. I'll get testimonials...
BEN	Maria...
MARIA	Listen to me. Your trial could become a rallying cry for Reform. Ben, you could turn this defeat into victory.
MACDONALD	(*returning*) Your companions inside have all signed.

SAM	They may do as they wish. (*passing the paper back to him*) I don't so easily put my name to a lie.
SARAH	Please, for Mamma's sake.
SAM	Sarah, this is for her sake, and for yours.
MACDONALD	I'm obliged to warn you that unless he has your signed confession this morning, the Chief Justice will see you punished to the full extent of the law.
SAM	My life's been on the line all along.
MACDONALD	Sir, the Crown will not only take your life. It will take the fruits of your lifetime's labour.
SAM	(*looking to BEN for confirmation*) Ben?
BEN	Confiscation, Sam. It's archaic...but it's still on the books.
MACDONALD	(*to SAM*) If you're found guilty, your family will be destitute. The house they live in, even the clothes on their back will be forfeit.
SARAH	(*turning to SAM, horrified*) Papa...did you know that?
SAM	No, lass. (*to MACDONALD*) but does this confession guarantee that won't happen?
MACDONALD	(*hesitating*) You have the word of the Chief Justice...
MARIA	You'll both be safe in the hands of the people. They'll know the truth when they hear it.
SARAH	(*to her*) You want your husband to risk hanging?
MARIA	It's less of a risk than trusting Robinson!
SARAH	The Chief Justice must be a man of honour!

MARIA   In a pig's eye!

MACDONALD   Madam!

BEN   Maria, please...(*leading her away from the others*)

MARIA   Ben, remember what he did to my family.

BEN   I know. But you must let people make their own decisions.

> *SARAH takes the paper from MACDONALD and holds it out to SAM.*

SARAH   Papa, I'm begging you, sign this paper...If you won't, I'll tell my sisters you don't care if you ever see them again...that you don't even care what becomes of them.

SAM   Give me the cursed thing.

> *MACDONALD passes SAM the pen. SAM signs, then passes the paper back to MACDONALD. He turns to SARAH and stares at her for a moment.*

SAM   (*quietly*) Lass, you had no need to speak to me so hard. (*turning his back and walking off*) Jailer, I'm going back to my cell.

> *MACDONALD comforts SARAH as he walks her to the exit.*

MARIA   (*to BEN*) How could she be so spineless?

BEN   Perhaps, Maria, she wants him alive. Perhaps she loves him enough not to care about defeats or victories.

> *SARAH exits. MACDONALD turns back to the WAITS.*

MARIA   My father would have disowned me if I'd asked him to betray his principles.

MACDONALD	(*crossing to them*) I'm offering you one last chance...
	BEN looks at MARIA, who stands resolved.
MACDONALD	Madam, I suspect your husband might wish to be sensible.
MARIA	My husband will act according to his conscience.
BEN	(*taking a breath, and looking at MARIA*) I fought against John Robinson's corruption and injustice, sir. I cannot say otherwise.
	This scene overlaps with the next one as ROBINSON enters another part of the stage and stands without acknowledging the scene around him. MACDONALD crosses to him and passes him a stack of papers - 27 of them, but he keeps JAKE's in his hand.
MARIA	Ben, I'm so proud of you!
BEN	As proud as you are of your father?
MARIA	Oh, yes...yes, I am.
	A passionate kiss. WHEELER moves in and rough handles MARIA away from BEN as ROBINSON reacts to MACDONALD's unheard report.
ROBINSON	Corruption and injustice, indeed!
WHEELER	(*to MARIA and BEN*) What do you think this is, a whore house?
	WHEELER drives MARIA off, still blowing joyful kisses to BEN. Then he and BEN exit as lights focus on ROBINSON alone. Others set up a campaign desk, a traveling case fitted as a bar, and a chair or two for:

Scene Five

ROBINSON'S TEMPORARY OFFICE IN NIAGARA

ROBINSON   (*to the audience*) I am accused of corruption because I would never allow hare-brained radicals to prevail over those who, by intellect, education and experience, are the most fit to guide this colony to its destiny. I am accused of tyranny because I quelled an uprising that would have imposed mob rule. Yesterday I thought our future as a nation founded on order and sound government was assured. Yet here I am, today, squaring off again. This time against two British Governors who have no more at stake in Upper Canada than they have knowledge of it. And this Benjamin Wait is about to play right into their hands. (*to MACDONALD, with a charming smile*) Good, Mr. MacDonald, twenty seven out of twenty nine is not a bad score.

MACDONALD   Twenty eight, sir. (*passing JAKE's confession*) I persuaded one to also confess to grand larceny.

ROBINSON   (*taking it*) You've been quite helpful.

MACDONALD   I was obliged to act in the interest of my client.

LUKIN enters.

ROBINSON   Yes?

LUKIN   I managed to ferret him out, father, from a tavern, I'm afraid.

ROBINSON   (*laying the papers down and dismissing MACDONALD*) Thank you, Mr. MacDonald.

MACDONALD   I'm only sorry I missed my chance to argue in front of you, sir.

MACNAB   (*off*) I don't give a fart how busy he is!

ROBINSON   I don't think you had much of a case.

MACDONALD   That's where you're wrong, sir. (*exiting*) If Mr. Chandler'd turned down your offer, I'd have pleaded him insane.

LUKIN   (*sitting*) A tad forward, isn't he?

ROBINSON   I'd say he has initiative. Don't sit down. I need the Sheriff to find all there is to find about Benjamin Wait.

LUKIN   Father...I was up half the night.

ROBINSON   That never bothers you when you're chasing women.

MACNAB   (*off*) He's not man enough to tell a knight of the realm to bide!

>*LUKIN exits, bumping into COLONEL ALLAN MACNAB of the Upper Canadian Militia.*

MACNAB   Canna ya watch out, laddie! (*to ROBINSON*) Well, Johnny, you better have good reason for hauling me away from my militia.

ROBINSON   I gather a toast is in order? (*pouring two drinks*) You are about to become "Sir Allan"?

MACNAB   Colonel Sir Allan MacNab...from the darling Victoria herself. The wee lassie knows who saved her from the republican hordes.

ROBINSON   Tell me, Sir Allan —

MACNAB   (*drinking*) Your brother's distillery throws out the scotch and bottles the piss.

ROBINSON   What do think is going to happen when the wee lassie discovers you told her a wee fib?

MACNAB	What fib?
ROBINSON	You had five hundred well-armed troops against how many farmers with muskets and pikes?
MACNAB	(*winking*) Ah, well, rebels are hard to count in the woods.
ROBINSON	The thirty short ones in blue were the rebels. The fifteen hundred tall ones in green were the trees.
MACNAB	I got the supplies I wanted, didn't I?
ROBINSON	You fooled Governor Arthur, but you can't expect to pull the wool over Lord Durham's eyes.
MACNAB	I don't give a fart for Lord Durham.
ROBINSON	He is the Queen's cousin.
MACNAB	Oh.
ROBINSON	And I hear they correspond.
MACNAB	(*beat*) She wouldn't take back my title, would she?
ROBINSON	You called the tune, Allan. The piper must be paid.
MACNAB	It's not the piper I'm worried about. It's my wife. I'd rather face the flames of hell.
ROBINSON	Then, admit you made an error. Or claim your clerk mixed up your figures. Do that, and I will personally intervene on your behalf.
MACNAB	(*incredulous*) You'll speak for me?
ROBINSON	As long as you make it clear to George Arthur that the majority of the population, including all settlers of substance and character support my administration.

MACNAB   You want me to say that all good settlers are
              happy to be ruled by John Beverley Robinson
              and his uncles and his brothers...(*as LUKIN
              returns*) and his son?

                          LUKIN repacks the "bar".

ROBINSON   For the good of your country. Because, you see,
              Durham not only has the power to take away
              your title. He has the power to redesign our
              entire political structure.

MACNAB   I don't give a fart for political structure.

ROBINSON   You'll give a fart if he puts us under the rule of
              Quebec.

MACNAB   I'll never give a fart for Quebec.

ROBINSON   If there is no more Upper Canada, there will be
              no more Upper Canadian militia.

MACNAB   Oh.

ROBINSON   Where will you be without your personal army?
              Back in the bush with no one to brawl with but
              Mrs. MacNab?

MACNAB   All right, but answer me this, if I haven't been
              fighting rebels, what in the hell *have* I been
              doing for the last eight months?

ROBINSON   Defending loyal colonists against American
              invaders. And you may boast of as many of those
              as you wish.

MACNAB   Oh, piss. Even a Brit isn't going to swallow
              that.

ROBINSON   I do have a hanged and quartered body to offer as
              evidence.

MACNAB   But he was the only Yankee in the pack!

ROBINSON	A pack...yes, a small pack of wastrels and vagabonds...misled by American cunning.
MACNAB	That's good, laddie. It might even work...if Sam Chandler weren't one of them.
LUKIN	(*a sudden memory*) Sarah Chandler!
ROBINSON	Don't interrupt.
MACNAB	(*to LUKIN*) Aye, you met her.
ROBINSON	What's this?
LUKIN	A girl who wrote to me, sir. She was at a ball with (*indicating MACNAB*) his daughter.
ROBINSON	(*to MACNAB*) You know this man?
MACNAB	I counted him a friend till he took a shot at me. Sam's one of the richest men in the Western district, not to mention Grand Master of the Orange Lodge. How d'ya expect to pull the wool over Durham's eyes about that?
ROBINSON	(*beat*) You take care of your wee fib, Allan. I'll take care of mine.
MACNAB	You know, I have a little canal scheme your bank might cast a kinder eye on.
ROBINSON	It's not my bank.
MACNAB	Johnny, you're the one calling the tune.
ROBINSON	I'll arrange a meeting when I'm back in Toronto.
MACNAB	And by the by, my wife might fancy an invitation to Toronto. A "lady" should have more to lord it over than the locals. (*exits*)
LUKIN	Having to call that ass Sir Allan will turn me into a republican.

ROBINSON   Don't you ever say that!

LUKIN   Oh, father...

ROBINSON   Have you forgotten it was Republicans drove
               your grandfather from Virginia!

LUKIN   With nothing but his British flag and a small
               chest of gold!

ROBINSON   There was no chest of gold! We had nothing left!

LUKIN   I'm sorry, sir.

ROBINSON   You may be. If the trials aren't over before
               Durham gets here, you may learn what havoc an
               unleashed mob can wreak.

LUKIN   I would like to help...it's just...all you let me do
               is run errands...

ROBINSON   (*beat*) This girl who wrote to you...

               *SARAH, with a magazine, and ANNIE
               enter another part of the stage as Scene
               Five and Scene Six overlap.*

ROBINSON   (*continued*)...did she mention if her father had a
               particular grudge against me?

LUKIN   She asked me to convince you he was innocent.
               If I'd been able to put her face to her name, I
               might have tried.

ROBINSON   Find his confession.

Scene Six

ANNIE'S BOARDING HOUSE

ANNIE	(*anxious*) You don't figure the Justice'll change his mind? That's not why your staying?
	LUKIN passes SAM's confession to ROBINSON .
SARAH	Of course not.
ROBINSON	(*tearing the confession in two*) A vagabond Grand Master won't wash.
LUKIN	Oh, hell, father.
SARAH	Mr. MacDonald is afraid my father will change his.
ROBINSON	MacDonald may get his chance...(*a memory stirs*) MacDonald...what was it that clever lad said?
LUKIN	Lord Durham is hardly going to ask for each rebel's community standing, is he?
ROBINSON	Tiny holes sink ships, particularly ships of state. Let's go see what the Sheriff's turned up...and after that, I'll set you a task you may actually enjoy.
	LUKIN picks up the "bar". The rest of Robinson's office should remain, and both men exit as LIZZIE enters.
LIZZIE	(*with a letter for SARAH*) Is it from your gentleman?
ANNIE	He remembered you?

SARAH   (*her face falling*) No. It's from my mother.

ANNIE   Now, miss, if she's coming here for the trial—

SARAH   Mr. Wait is the only one on trial! (*opening it*)
             Papa and the others just get sentenced, remember.

ANNIE   Then if she's coming for the sentence, she's
             going to have to share your bed.

SARAH   (*scanning it*) She isn't. (*a touch of bitterness*)
             She's leaving the matter entirely in my hands.

ANNIE   Oh. Well, miss, you can't blame her for being
             mad. I was fit to be tied when Jake's Da ran off
             to fight Napoleon.

SARAH   Mamma is not "fit to be tied". She's in a state of
             collapse.

ANNIE   (*wistfully*) A state of collapse. I couldn't afford
             that. But I'd have killed him with my bare hands,
             if the French hadn't done it for me. I learned my
             lesson though...I never got married again. What
             little I got stays safe in my name.

             ANNIE exits.

SARAH   (*to LIZZIE*) You told me your father was in
             Belgium...Did he die in the battle of Waterloo?

             *LIZZIE nods, SARAH does a mental
             calculation, possibly aided by fingers, then
             draws away from LIZZIE sharply.*

SARAH   Oh, that woman!

LIZZIE   (*alarmed by her tone*) You fit to be tied?

SARAH   (*sorry for her*) Oh, you poor child. I can't blame
             you. (*to soothe LIZZIE's feelings she shows her
             the magazine*) Look what I bought to help me
             pass the next few days. (*flipping through the
             magazine*) Do you know why *The Albion* is so

SARAH   (*continued*) expensive? The people who publish
                    it employ men with carrier pigeons to travel on
                    big ships, and when only half way across the
                    ocean, they tie the news to the pigeon's legs and
                    fly them to New York where the magazine is
                    printed.

LIZZIE   (*laughing*) That's silly.

SARAH   No, it's very smart. Otherwise we'd have to wait
                    till the big ships arrive to see what ladies are
                    wearing in England.

LIZZIE   (*showing her a picture*) See.

SARAH   Yes...that's the governor of Quebec! (*reading*)
                    Oh! He'll be here on Friday! Do you know what
                    you do if an Earl looks at you?

LIZZIE   Wiggle your figure?

SARAH   No, dear, no. (*demonstrating curtsey*) You put
                    one leg behind the other...

                         LIZZIE imitates her, awkwardly. MARIA
                         enters with the baby, and her second pair
                         of boots.

MARIA   Miss Chandler, what nonsense are you teaching
                    that girl!

SARAH   To act like a lady, Mrs. Wait, Perhaps that's why
                    you don't recognize the lesson.

LIZZIE   (*bringing the magazine to MARIA*) See the
                    pretty governor.

MARIA   (*pushing it away*) Pretty? I heard he hanged six
                    hundred men!

SARAH   I'm surprised someone so up on politics can't tell
                    the governor of Upper Canada from the governor
                    of Lower.

MARIA   (*caught out*) Well...One's a butcher and one's a
         fop. Neither have anything to do with us, Lizzie,
         so how about taking Augusta? I need to go sell
         my boots.

         LIZZIE takes the baby.

SARAH   The pretty man is the Queen's cousin, Lizzie. It's
         a great honour to have him visit our colony.

MARIA   Lizzie, our *country* will soon have a parliament
         of it's own. Then there'll be no fops or butchers.

SARAH   We already have a parliament, Lizzie, and —

MARIA   We have a legislative assembly! With as much
         power as Augusta asleep in your arms! But when
         Robinson falls, we'll have a democracy. Your
         pretty Queen's cousin will be out on his ear!

SARAH   Mrs. Wait!

MARIA   Believe me, Lizzie...we're going to see the
         Republic of Canada yet!

SARAH   You're worse than a rebel! You're an out and out
         traitor!

ANNIE   (*entering, with a card for SARAH*) He's here,
         Miss Chandler. He's at the door!

         SARAH glances at the note, and runs out.

ANNIE   (*to MARIA, as soon as SARAH has cleared*)
         You better collect your child and hightail it, girl.

MARIA   What's wrong?

ANNIE   You stole that watch, didn't you?

MARIA   Of course I didn't.

ANNIE	Well, you done something! Because there's two men out there. The nob for that snippet. And the Sheriff, come to collect you! (*as MARIA strides past ANNIE*) Not that way...use the back door. Where are you going...Mrs. Wait!
	ANNIE and LIZZIE with the baby follow MARIA off as SARAH and LUKIN enter.

Scene Seven

A RIVER BANK

LUKIN	Forgotten? I've been dreaming of that dance every night since.
SARAH	(*a little nervous*) Susie is still annoyed that you danced with me and not her.
LUKIN	If only I'd remembered you were with the MacNabs —but you cast such a spell, Susan vanished from my mind...
SARAH	You're very kind, Lukin.
LUKIN	I'm so glad I've found you...I'm almost thankful for your father's rebellion. (*moving closer to her, causing her to move away slightly*) Though, you know, his treason is going to ruin everything for us.
SARAH	For "us"?
LUKIN	Well, yes. Can you imagine what mother would say if I brought you home for tea?
SARAH	Would you want to?

LUKIN	Oh, Sarah...I never want to let you out of my sight again. But society will see you only as a criminal's daughter.
SARAH	Lukin...I'm not the traitor...
LUKIN	It's so unfair...
SARAH	I'm devoted to the Queen!
LUKIN	How could your father have done this to us..?
SARAH	I don't know.
LUKIN	Sarah, you don't suppose — Would it be possible that Mr. Chandler was insane?
SARAH	There's no insanity in my family!
LUKIN	But he might have suffered - oh - some sort of stroke that damaged his brain?
SARAH	What do you mean?
LUKIN	You wrote that he was a loving husband and parent.What man in his right mind would risk his wife and children for a lost cause?
SARAH	I saw him in jail. He was fine.
LUKIN	No, try to understand what I'm saying to you. If, when he joined the rebels, Samuel Chandler was the victim of a mental aberration...he could be judged "not responsible for his actions".
SARAH	(*moving*) I'll ask my lawyer.
LUKIN	It was MacDonald's idea ...in a way. Sarah, there'll be no disgrace for anyone.
SARAH	(*beat*) What would happen to Papa?
LUKIN	Well...I guess he'd be released to your custody.

SARAH   Then...I should make him say he had a stroke?

LUKIN   No, no. You need other people to declare him insane. I'm sure Colonel MacNab will volunteer. And I bet your other neighbours would sign a declaration if they knew it would help you?

SARAH   I'll send a message home at once.

LUKIN   No, let me draw up the document.

SARAH   Lukin, I'm so grateful.

LUKIN   I'll arrange a courier as well.

SARAH   I only hope, someday, I can repay your generosity.

LUKIN   Oh, you'll have your chance. As soon as our troubles are over. (*beat*) I just wish you could solve my problems as easily as I solved yours.

SARAH   I wish I could too.

LUKIN   Well...actually...I noticed you're staying at the same house as Benjamin Wait's wife?

SARAH   Yes, worse luck.

LUKIN   Has she said anything to you? Anything that might be of use against her husband?

SARAH   If you want my opinion, she's the one you should put on trial.

LUKIN   Give me some evidence, we'll try them both.

SARAH   Oh...I didn't mean that. She has a baby, you know.

LUKIN   Sarah, I thought you were devoted to the Queen?

SARAH   Well...Lukin, I think she was making it up...

LUKIN	I thought you wanted to help me.
SARAH	(*beat*) Mrs. Wait wrote a letter about Americans invading us. I saw her pass it to her husband in jail.
LUKIN	Oh, you sweetheart! Look, I have to run. But I'll see you again...(*kissing her aggressively, then running off*) I intend to collect on your gratitude.

> *SARAH looks after him, her hand to her mouth. Then she exits as ROBINSON ushers MARIA into:*

Scene Eight & Scene Nine

> *The next two scenes overlap, Scene Eight at ROBINSON office and Scene Nine at ANNIE's house.*

ROBINSON'S TEMPORARY OFFICE

ROBINSON	Mrs. Wait, are you, by any chance, an adulteress?
MARIA	(*gasping*) How dare you!
ROBINSON	I'm simply curious as to why you're so anxious to become a widow.
MARIA	(*beat*) Even you, sir, are powerless to hang a man once a jury has set him free.
ROBINSON	(*laughing*) You're a daughter of Reform, all right...Oh, yes, Maria Randal, even if the Sheriff hadn't told me, I'd recognize that fanatical gleam, that strident tone — and above all, that naive determination to invest twelve good men and true with your own ruthless agenda.

MARIA	You know whose daughter I am, and you call me ruthless?
ROBINSON	Your father was my opponent in politics and I defeated him by political means. Yet, as you must know, he never considered resorting to guns.
MARIA	That's why the people still have no voice in their government. I don't share my father's scruples. If I had a gun, I'd shoot you where you stand.
ROBINSON	You make me tremble, madam. You personify the violence I knew his liberalism would breed.
MARIA	It's your tyranny that has bred violence.
ROBINSON	Had I been tyrannical enough to silence Robert Randal before his contempt for authority had a chance to spread, there never would have been a rebellion in Upper Canada. Your little daughter would not be in danger of losing her father at a more tender age than you lost yours.
MARIA	My God, you have no shame...
ROBINSON	If your husband insists on a trial, she won't be left with the illusion that he's a hero. He'll be revealed for exactly what he is - an irresponsible wastrel who seized upon the rebellion to avoid being imprisoned for debt.
MARIA	That's a lie!
ROBINSON	(*producing two papers*) I have a Sheriff's order for the repossession of your house, and a deposition from a solicitor who dismissed your husband for negligence.
MARIA	And I have the date of his dismissal! The same day he stood at the poll and spoke the Reform candidate's name! His employer threw him out without even the wages he had coming! I have records of his attempts to sue. I have proof you

MARIA   (*continued*) ordered your magistrates to throw out any case brought by a Reformer! The world is going to hear chapter and verse on your abuse of office!

ROBINSON   (*pause*) Ben Wait took the law into his own hands. No jury will shed tears for him.

MARIA   Then why did you bring me here? Why did you let the women into the jail? You expected to bully us more easily than men, didn't you?

LUKIN   (*bursting in*) Father...Oh, am I interrupting?

ROBINSON   Mrs. Wait, let me make your choice clear to you. Either you take my offer back to your husband and prevail on him to accept it, or I will hang him.

MARIA   What you have made clear to me, Mr. Robinson, is that there's a noose around your neck too. I only pray it's my husband's testimony that slams the trap from under your feet. (*exiting*)

LUKIN   (*letting out a breath*) Was that Maria Wait?

ROBINSON   Her father will never be dead while she's alive. (*beat*) I wish my own immortality were so assured.

LUKIN   If that's a dig at me, you're not being fair.

ROBINSON   Perhaps not. Lukin, I'm in more difficulty than I thought.

LUKIN   Well, sir, after I completed my assignment, I dropped by the jail. (*passing MARIA's letter*) This may alleviate the problem you obviously failed to solve.

> ROBINSON *reads as LUKIN smiles and*
> SARAH *enters. Segue into Scene Nine.*

ANNIE'S HOUSE

SARAH	(*to the audience*) I suppose I could look after Augusta...since it's my fault...no, it's hers. She wrote the stupid thing. (*as MARIA enters*) Oh, thank heaven...(*as MARIA looks at her*) Mrs. Beemer said you'd been arrested.
MARIA	(*going on*) She must be worried to death...
SARAH	Mrs. Wait...(*as MARIA turns*) Is there anything new about your husband's case?
MARIA	Mr. Robinson gave me more proof that I was right. You know, you still have time to let your Papa change his mind.
SARAH	Papa is as good as free. It's Mr. Wait I'm concerned about.
MARIA	Ben's life is safe in the hands of the people.
SARAH	The people! What people? People like Mrs. Beemer? People who sell a gold watch for less than one week's lodging?
MARIA	That was the Tories' fault. Everybody's so poor she couldn't get a good price.
SARAH	So you sold your boots and gave her that money too! Any fool can see she's stolen your watch —
MARIA	Miss Chandler!
SARAH	(*over MARIA's protest*) — the same way her son stole that thousand dollars!
MARIA	It's a shame and a sin to defame a good woman without an iota of proof.
SARAH	Do good woman have illegitimate children? I can prove she has!
MARIA	I don't believe you!

SARAH	Her husband was killed at Waterloo. Wasn't that 1815?
MARIA	So?
SARAH	Lizzie! She's nowhere near twenty three. (*beat*) How's that for shame and sin, for you?
MARIA	(*beat, weakly*) All right, but you have no idea of how hard her life may have been...
SARAH	My point is you trust Mrs. Beemer because she's poor. The reason she's poor is that she's dirty, lazy and completely without morals. You don't trust Mr. Robinson because he's achieved the highest office in the colony. It makes no sense, no sense at all!
MARIA	(*beat*) He murdered my father.
SARAH	What? No...
MARIA	Oh, not with a knife or a bullet...but he murdered him all the same. He wasn't content with destroying him politically. He stripped him of everything he owned. He hounded him out of his country. It's an awful thing to watch someone you love die in exile, with only his failures to list on his grave. I have no choice but to oppose John Robinson, Miss Chandler, because I know I can never appease him. And mark my words, you'll rue the day you ever delivered your father into his power.

MARIA exits. SARAH exits.

ROBINSON'S OFFICE

LUKIN	Shall I order her arrested?
ROBINSON	(*looking up from the letter, happily*) Pardon..? No, she's not worth the bother. (*collecting all the papers*) Lukin, thanks to you, we can pack up the Niagara office. Actually, you may go home if you want.

LUKIN   (*thinking of SARAH*) Not yet! I feel I should wait till you're finished in court.

> *Lights focus on ROBINSON. He moves downstage with the papers and addresses the audience while the Niagara office is struck. LUKIN follows to stand just outside the spotlight.*

ROBINSON   What happens in court is of little concern. Entered into evidence: twenty seven confessions, (*passing them to LUKIN*) one petition of insanity. (*passing it to LUKIN*) And the trial of one misguided hero, whom I let attack me to his heart's content. There wasn't time to hand down sentences, but they'll all be short ones. Even Ben Wait's. It's the quickest way to sweep him under the rug.

LUKIN   Father...how come the prosecution didn't mention her letter?

ROBINSON   (*smiling, to LUKIN*) Come along with me tomorrow, my boy. (*putting MARIA'S letter in his own pocket*) Watch me make real capital of the opportunity you've handed me.

Scene Ten

NEAR & ABOARD LORD DURHAM'S BOAT, AT NIAGARA

> *Lights change to indicate morning on the full stage with the sound of Niagara Falls in the distance.*
>
> *A SAILOR enters and stands "at ease". GOVERNOR ARTHUR enters and crosses toward him. The SAILOR snaps*

> *to attention. He could pipe ARTHUR*
> *aboard - bosun's whistle not bagpipe.*

ARTHUR (*looking around*) There is no one on this desk.

ROBINSON (*to LUKIN*) Say nothing unless spoken to and don't let on that you're my son.

> *ROBINSON and LUKIN follow*
> *ARTHUR aboard.*

ROBINSON Your excellency, I trust you brought MacNab's revised statement?

ARTHUR I see no need to mention that today.

ROBINSON But it proves you have your colony under control, sir. Don't you wish the Durham Report to give the credit to you?

> *COLONEL COUPER of the 92nd*
> *Highlanders enters.*

COUPER Your Excellency, sorry to keep you cooling your heels. (*to the SAILOR*) Dismissed! (*to ARTHUR*) I'm Charles Couper, secretary to His Lordship.

> *The SAILOR exits.*

ARTHUR Colonel Couper.

COUPER Not a bad colony for you, eh? Not as good as India, of course. I read your wife's a bit upset.

ARTHUR (*beat*) I trust Lord Durham's delay is not occasioned by anything serious.

COUPER Had an impulse to go sight-seeing at dawn. I warned him he'd get a headache. Doctor's giving him a laudanum dose again...

> *DURHAM enters.*

DURHAM	Ah, Sir George...good of you to come from Torwhatnot to meet me.
ARTHUR	I am honoured to extend my —
DURHAM	(*cutting him off*) I visited the cataract this morning, the mighty falls of Niagara. Could you imagine such a rampage of power, such a relentless force? Or are they old hat to you by now?
ARTHUR	Unordered nature is not to my taste, my lord.
DURHAM	But don't our pretensions to order seem petty beside that torrent? Is it any wonder the inhabitants rose up against us when the very nature of this land declares for liberty? You won't have heard yet, Sir George, I've proclaimed an amnesty for the rebels of Lower Canada. I intend to do the same for the rebels here.
ARTHUR	May I ask with what authority you issue a proclamation in my domain?
DURHAM	(*surprised*) Haven't you received orders to defer to me as Governor General of both Canadas?
ARTHUR	I have not.
COUPER	Oops.
DURHAM	Tardy though it may be, a dispatch to that effect should be even now coursing the waves.
ROBINSON	My lord, does London intend Upper Canada's (*indicating ARTHUR*) most able Governor to be demoted?
DURHAM	Who are you?
ARTHUR	(*snapping*) You asked me to bring the Chief Justice.

DURHAM	Ah, yes...the man who underestimates discontent.
ROBINSON	I have underestimated nothing, sir.
DURHAM	Is there not an army of honest settlers testifying otherwise even as we speak?
ROBINSON	We have twenty nine prisoners remaining.
DURHAM	(*looking at ARTHUR*) Am I to take it that fourteen hundred and seventy one have been executed?
ROBINSON	Only one, sir...(*looking at ARTHUR*) and...
DURHAM	And?
ARTHUR	Ah...happily...the earlier intelligence turned out to be a clerical error.
ROBINSON	(*quickly to head off DURHAM's explosion*) However, my lord, if rebel testimony is of interest, my assistant has the court records for your perusal.

LUKIN presents papers to DURHAM who puts his hands behind his back.

DURHAM	Coups.
COUPER	(*reaching for them, and reading from the first*) "Our uprising was rash and unprovoked"... (*shuffling through them*) "We were terribly misled."
DURHAM	Misled?
COUPER	(*shuffling*) "I joined for the chance to steal Martin Overholt's thousand dollars" (*shuffling*) "Only a state of lunacy could have made a well-to-do man fall prey to Yankee Notions."
DURHAM	Is that how you term liberty, a 'Yankee Notion'?

ROBINSON   No, sir. It's how I term armed insurrection.

ARTHUR   (*to ROBINSON, pleasantly surprised*) Well said, Mr. Robinson.

ROBINSON   (*bowing to him*) Thank you, sir.

DURHAM   Are there no honest rebels at all?

ARTHUR   Only thieves and lunatics are discontent in my colony.

COUPER   Oh, this sounds more like it - "Men of conscience had only one choice..."

DURHAM   (*taking the letter from him*)..."to abandon their country, or do battle for it. The Chief Justice may manipulate facts, but honest souls will know the truth. I ask you to pass judgment not on me, but on ...(*looking at ROBINSON*) John Beverly Robinson, for it is the despot, not the patriot, who should be in chains before you." (*folding the letter and ostentatiously putting it in his pocket*) So...whom shall be found guilty? Him or you?

ROBINSON   The jury has found. They did not condone violence.

DURHAM   Even though a man of conscience had no choice?

ROBINSON   (*smiling*) I have another document which may put his rhetoric into perspective.

          LUKIN passes the paper to DURHAM.
          MARIA enters a neutral area.

DURHAM   "Dearest Ben...(*turning it over*) Your loving Maria." Am I to read a woman's billet-doux?

ROBINSON   The relevant lines are underscored.

DURHAM   But the irrelevant ones...

MARIA	I could bear to be without you while our baby was inside me. Now, my body aches for yours every night and all day too. I comfort myself that the desire burning...
DURHAM	(*enjoying himself*) I hope she and "dearest Ben" are married?
ROBINSON	(*shrugging*) If you recognize Methodist rite.
DURHAM	...desire burning in me...
MARIA	...is nothing to the desire burning in our country. Soon ten thousand Patriots will make our dreams come true!
DURHAM	(*aloud, in unison*) Ten thousand Patriots will make our dreams come true?
MARIA	President Van Buren is on the verge of giving us full military support!
DURHAM	He wouldn't dare!
ROBINSON	The president is up for re-election. The majority of Americans believe they have a divine right to overrun the continent. In fact, an American led this handful of hooligans.
DURHAM	(*to COUPER*) You'd best look into it.
ROBINSON	(*pressing his real point*) Whether the threat materializes or not, your lordship must realize that those, like Ben Wait, who attack our system of government, are not men of conscience.
ARTHUR	I'm convinced they're foreign spies.
ROBINSON	(*to DURHAM*) If you wish more proof, read the rest of that letter.

MARIA (*as DURHAM returns to the letter*) Soon you and our country will shake off our British shackles. Soon we'll no more be ruled by a slip of a girl! (*exits*)

DURHAM A slip of a girl?

COUPER She can't mean ...(*he daren't say it*)

ROBINSON The Queen? Oh yes, she does.

DURHAM A slip of a girl!

ARTHUR (*to DURHAM*) Your amnesty is not the remedy called for here.

DURHAM For her, no! I'd choke her myself! But, for the rest...your famous severity won't help matters either.

ARTHUR If you're referring to *The Albion*, that story is slander. There were only two hundred and forty executions in my last regime.

COUPER (*ironic*) Is that all?

ARTHUR Colonel!

DURHAM Be content with the one you already killed, Sir George. I will tolerate no more of your sanguinary measures.

ARTHUR Until the dispatch that should be even now coursing the waves arrives, I am not accountable to you! Not for my previous post, and not for this one!

COUPER Never see the Taj Mahal that way.

ARTHUR Colonel Couper!

DURHAM Don't shout, damn you!

ARTHUR   (*to DURHAM*) I will tolerate no interference
         from you!

DURHAM   (*losing control*) I have left Quebec in a time of
         crises. I have travelled seven hundred miles on
         your horrible little boats, on those rolling logs
         you call roads! I have been choked by dust,
         drenched by thunder storms, devoured by
         mosquitoes!

COUPER   (*as a warning*) Remember your head, my lord.

DURHAM   Yes, and I have a headache! All because you
         promised me the testimony of fifteen hundred
         rebels to incorporate into my report. Now I find I
         have made this journey for a clerical error, and
         (*viciously*) the chance to be insulted by a
         butcher!

                  DURHAM and COUPER exit. ARTHUR,
                  ROBINSON and LUKIN move in the
                  opposite direction.

ROBINSON   Your Excellency must complain to London. You
           must demand that madman be recalled.

ARTHUR   I will do that - and more. Mr. Robinson...John, I
         need your cooperation.

                  MACDONALD enters carrying a judge's
                  robe.

ROBINSON   You have it, sir.

ARTHUR   We hold about thirty prisoners? It wouldn't take
         many to make the point.

ROBINSON   What point?

ARTHUR   That Durham and his amnesty both be damned.

ROBINSON   (*dismayed*) I see...

LUKIN   (*alarmed*) Father...

ROBINSON	(*glancing at LUKIN*) Very clever, sir...except I...
ARTHUR	What's this?
ROBINSON	(*making a decision*) Nothing, sir.
LUKIN	Father, tell him.
ROBINSON	(*donning the robe*) Does Your Excellency have a preference?

> *ROBINSON moves to the position of JUDGE. He addresses unseen prisoners in the dock.*

Scene Eleven

A COURTROOM IN NIAGARA.

ARTHUR	The thief...
ROBINSON	Jacob Beemer,

> *ANNIE enters.*

ARTHUR	...and the spy of course...
ROBINSON	Benjamin Wait,

> *MARIA enters.*

ARTHUR	Oh...the lunatic, perhaps. (*exiting*) His existence is useless anyway.
ROBINSON	And Samuel Chandler.

> *SARAH enters.*

LUKIN	Tell him you promised mercy!
ROBINSON	For you three men there can be no mercy. You will be taken from this court to the place from which you last came, and there remain until the twenty-fifth of August, when, at the stroke of noon, you shall be hanged by the neck until you are dead.
SARAH	(*screaming*) No...no...you promised!
ROBINSON	And your bodies shall be quartered.
MARIA	(*shouting*) You'll never hang my husband. I won't let you!

Black out. End of Act One.

Act Two, Scene One

A COURT ROOM IN NIAGARA AND OUTSIDE

> *A GUARD and WHEELER stand on duty. The WOMEN are in the same places as at the end of Act One, except they now face the audience. ROBINSON faces off stage.*

MARIA   (*to the audience*) Saturday, August eleventh. Twenty-six other rebels were sentenced to a year in jail...and then...

ROBINSON   ...for you three men there can be no mercy.

SARAH   (*to the audience*) Not Papa...no, there's been a mistake...

ROBINSON   ...until the twenty-fifth of August,

MARIA   (*to the audience*) Two weeks. I only have two weeks!

ROBINSON   When at the stroke of noon.

SARAH   (*to the audience*) My mother...my sisters...

> *ROBINSON and the WOMEN turn so they are looking straight at each other.*

ROBINSON   ...be hanged by the neck until you are dead.

SARAH   No...no...you promised!

ROBINSON   And your bodies shall be quartered.

MARIA   You'll never hang my husband. I won't let you!

>   *As ROBINSON takes off the robe,*
>   *MARIA runs toward him shouting the*
>   *second verse of " Up and Waur'em Willie."*

MARIA   "Better brave the tyrant's frown
Then see the country fall —

ANNIE   (*shouting*) Be quiet, girl.

MARIA   (*in his face*) Bare corruption's filthy breast
And make the people see —

ANNIE   (*moving to her*) For the love of God...

>   *THE GUARD and WHEELER try to grab*
>   *MARIA. She wrestles free enough to*
>   *continue her song.*

MARIA   The vile, the base, the selfish nest
That feeds on such as we."

ANNIE   You want your child to lose her mother too!

>   *MARIA stops struggling. The GUARD*
>   *and WHEELER force MARIA and ANNIE*
>   *out of ROBINSON's way. They hold the*
>   *WOMEN back as ROBINSON moves*
>   *toward the exit. MACDONALD blocks*
>   *his path.*

MACDONALD   Sir, I don't understand...

ROBINSON   I said there was a chance of mercy, never a
certainty. (*dismissing MACDONALD, to*
LUKIN) Our boat is waiting.

>   *MACDONALD steps back, ROBINSON*
>   *heads off, but is stopped by LUKIN.*

LUKIN	Sir, Sarah's father...
ROBINSON	I need the Governor on my side. Durham would have believed every lie the rebels told!
LUKIN	After today, I'm not so sure they were lying.
ROBINSON	Lukin!
LUKIN	Father, I don't want to be your assistant anymore.
ROBINSON	(*beat*) If you haven't the stomach for office, you can do without its privileges. You may start by taking public transportation home.

> *ROBINSON exits. THE GUARD exits after him. SARAH crosses to LUKIN.*

SARAH	You lied to me! Your father lied!

> *MACDONALD follows her and grabs her arm.*

MACDONALD	(*pulling her away*) Miss Chandler, don't!
LUKIN	(*at the same time*) Please, Sarah...please...
SARAH	(*to MacDonald*) But you know they did!
LUKIN	It wasn't my fault.

> *LUKIN sits on the ground as MACDONALD takes SARAH downstage.*

MACDONALD	Listen, the sentence can be commuted. But the Governor will rely on Robinson's advice. No matter how badly they've treated you, you can't afford to antagonize him or his son.
SARAH	(*pausing*) What about my family?
MACDONALD	If I can keep your father from hanging, I'll have all the time in the world to fight confiscation.

SARAH	(*gazing up at him*) And if you can't?
MACDONALD	The Crown won't re-open a case after the criminal's been executed.
SARAH	Mr. MacDonald...is there nothing I can do?
MACDONALD	Go home and make preparations for the worst. I'll try to stop it from happening. (*offering his hand, as he might at a funeral*) In case we don't meet again, I wish you the very, very best of luck.

> *MACDONALD exits. SARAH stares after him. MARIA crosses to her. There's still tension between the women. They maintain some physical distance.*

MARIA	What does your lawyer advise?
SARAH	(*a brief hesitation before confiding in MARIA*) That I ready my family to be put out on the streets.
ANNIE	(*from her position*) That'll be an education for you.
MARIA	(*shocked*) Mrs. Beemer...
ANNIE	(*to MARIA*) She always thought she was better than me. (*to SARAH*) Miss, let me tell you something. When my man ran off, I bundled my boys into the hold of a ship. Liam perished on the crossing, and when we got to Antigonish, the authorities didn't like the look of Tom's tongue. But Jake and me never went on the streets. And him being dead won't put Lizzie on the streets either.
MARIA	(*crossing to ANNIE*) Jake isn't dead yet!
ANNIE	He will be in two weeks.
MARIA	A lot can happen before then.

SARAH	What about the Americans you spoke of..?
MARIA	They may not come in time. Didn't MacDonald have any ideas?
SARAH	He's appealing to the man you called 'The Butcher'.
ANNIE	The one that hanged a thousand men?
MARIA	What about your Queen's cousin?
SARAH	He's not our governor.
MARIA	He might be able to help us.
ANNIE	Why would he bother?
SARAH	He did look kind...But he's gone back to Quebec...
MARIA	Then I'll go after him.
SARAH	(*beat*) I'll go too!
ANNIE	(*weighing SARAH's chances*) Now you might be talking...
MARIA	My God, I have no money!
SARAH	I can pay for you.
ANNIE	It's ten minutes to the last ferry!
MARIA	(*starting off*) Then come on.
SARAH	Hold your horses. How could we make sure he'd receive us?
MARIA	Oh, we can worry about that on the way.
ANNIE	(*to SARAH*) Like I said, miss, neither prince nor pauper...

> *SARAH turns and sees LUKIN. She looks back to ANNIE. An idea glimmers.*

MARIA (*impatient*) We have to fetch Augusta.

SARAH You get her —

ANNIE (*overlapping, to MARIA*) The little mite?

SARAH — I'll meet you at the pier.

ANNIE (*following MARIA off*) A trip like that! The child would die!

> *SARAH waits till they've cleared, then walks to where LUKIN is sitting.*

SARAH Lukin...

LUKIN (*feeling sorry for himself*) Neither of us has been lucky in our choice of fathers, you know.

SARAH Lukin, I'm sorry I accused you of lying.

LUKIN I meant most of what I said. Honestly.

SARAH I suppose I can't expect you to forgive me...

LUKIN Me...forgive you?

SARAH There's no excuse for my railing at you the way I did...

LUKIN Well...it wasn't very fair.

SARAH I'll always be grateful for what you tried to do for me.

LUKIN Do you mean that? Look, I don't have to go back to Toronto right away.

SARAH But I do...I'm on my way to Quebec City...

LUKIN To Lord Durham? (*laughing*) Oh, that's rich!

SARAH	You think it's hopeless?
LUKIN	No, it's perfect! Absolutely perfect!
SARAH	Lukin, how could I gain access to him?
LUKIN	You need the correct credentials, that's all...
SARAH	Would you write an introduction for me?
LUKIN	Oh, I'm not important enough...
SARAH	You're the most important young man in the colony, aren't you?
LUKIN	Well...I suppose.
SARAH	Please...I've no one else to turn to.
LUKIN	(*an idea forming*) I could use the official seal...(*rejecting the thought*) but I couldn't.
SARAH	I'd be so grateful...
LUKIN	(*shaking his head*) If father found out...
SARAH	Lukin, you can't imagine how grateful I'd be.
LUKIN	Do you mean that?
SARAH	(*beat*) Yes...
LUKIN	Truly?

SARAH kisses him.

LUKIN	I still have the key to father's desk...(*the ferry whistle blows*) The steamship leaves Queen's Quay in the morning. We'll have the ferry ride and the whole night together.
SARAH	Suppose I meet you in Toronto..?
LUKIN	Why? Nobody will see us.

SARAH	I have to go with...somebody else.
LUKIN	Who?
SARAH	Just...another woman.
LUKIN	You don't mean Maria Wait! Sarah, after that letter, she's the only person in the world Durham wants to hang!
SARAH	He read it?
LUKIN	You have to get rid of her, sweetheart! That traitorous bitch will sink any chance you have.
	Ferry whistle blows.
SARAH	She can't come with me unless I pay her fare!
MARIA	(*off*) Miss Chandler?
SARAH	Hurry, Lukin. We can get aboard before she catches us.
	SARAH takes his hand. They run off as the whistle of the ferry is superseded by the horn of a large ship.

Scene Two

THE LADIES' CABIN ON THE STEAMSHIP *ST. GEORGE*

> *Benches are set as a PURSER enters with a brass hand bell. MRS. MOODIE, an Englishwoman, enters, followed by her maid, PEGGY.*

PURSER	Sunday morning. Too damn early after Saturday night. Aboard the *S.S. St. George* out of Toronto. Bound for Kingston. We put chairs out on deck when it's fine. Raining cats and dogs today. (*to MRS. MOODIE*) Nice and dry in here, ma'am. (*as MRS. MOODIE sits*) If I might trouble you for your five dollars.
MRS. MOODIE	Five dollars!
PURSER	It be highway robbery, I know, but there be no highway.
MRS. MOODIE	(*giving him money*) How much for my maid?
PURSER	Same fare.
MRS. MOODIE	Are there no classes on this boat?
PURSER	In the first go off you're aboard a *ship*. In the second, you're in the Canadas. We have Upper and Lower of them, and that's trouble enough.

*SARAH enters, carrying a new, small
traveling bag, and perhaps wearing a new
collar or scarf.*

PURSER	Five dollars, miss.
SARAH	(*surprised*) Five dollars!
PURSER	We supply lunch, dinner and breakfast in the saloon and (*indicating bell*) my own humble self at your beck and call.

SARAH opens her bag and pays.

PEGGY	Look, ma'am! They're untying the ropes!
MRS. MOODIE	Don't fall out the porthole, Peggy.

> *The PURSER tips his cap and exits.*
> *SARAH sits. MRS. MOODIE sizes her*
> *up and decides to smile. SARAH ignores*
> *her. She takes out an official looking*
> *letter, then puts it back and takes out* The
> Albion. *She closes her bag, but doesn't*
> *put it down. We hear shouts of 'All*
> *aboard' off.*

MRS. MOODIE   Pardon me, is that the new *Albion*?

SARAH   It's last week's.

MRS. MOODIE   Old news then. (*beat*) Are you by any chance a
resident of Kingston?

SARAH   No, I'm not.

PEGGY   We're moving there.

MRS. MOODIE   (*to SARAH*) My husband, Major Moodie, has
been appointed Sheriff. For his loyal service to
the Crown. You may have heard of his exploits?

SARAH   I don't think so..

MRS. MOODIE   (*moving to sit beside her*) He and Colonel
MacNab captured a whole company of traitors.

PEGGY   They're taking up the gangplank.

MRS. MOODIE   I shan't be sorry to see the last of Toronto.
Although I regret missing the Robinsons' ball
next Friday. To my mind, Beverley House is the
only graceful residence in this benighted colony.

SARAH   Yes...it's quite imposing.

MRS. MOODIE   You've walked by it, I suppose.

SARAH   As a matter of fact, I was a guest there last night.

MRS. MOODIE   You don't say.

PEGGY	We're away from the pier!
SARAH	I'll miss the ball too...but there'll be plenty of others.
MRS. MOODIE	Ah, but Emma has managed a coup this time. The Governor himself will attend.
SARAH	Not Lord Durham?
MRS. MOODIE	Sir George Arthur.
PEGGY	There's a woman missed the boat!
MRS. MOODIE	He comes from the same part of England as I do.
PEGGY	She's running!
MRS. MOODIE	Peggy!
PEGGY	She's going to jump!
MRS. MOODIE	Peggy! (*to SARAH*) I don't know what gets into that class when they cross the Atlantic. (*beat*) May I ask how it is you are travelling without a servant?
SARAH	Oh...I...
MRS. MOODIE	I take it...you are a gentlewoman?
SARAH	Of course, Mrs...
MRS. MOODIE	...Moodie.
SARAH	I...I set out with a trusted maid. But she became ill...and, though the poor soul protested bitterly, I was forced to leave her behind.
MRS. MOODIE	Your journey must be of an urgent nature..?

SARAH My dear Papa has been wounded. Colonel Chandler was also performing loyal service for the Crown...in Quebec.

MARIA enters.

PEGGY She made it!

SARAH You!

MARIA (*out of breath*) Yes, I imagine you're surprised to see me.

MRS. MOODIE The good soul has recovered!

SARAH How did you get to Toronto?

MARIA On the cargo end of the same ferry you did.

SARAH Oh.

MARIA Along side the hens and sheep!

MRS. MOODIE No wonder she was ill.

SARAH Oh, no. This isn't my maid.

MARIA What maid?

SARAH Mrs. Wait...I didn't mean to leave you stranded.

MARIA What were you doing with John Robinson's son?

SARAH ...I beg your pardon?

MARIA I saw you! Arm in arm on the deck above me!

SARAH grabs the bell and rings it furiously.

MRS. MOODIE Why is this woman shouting!

MARIA (*to SARAH*) What are you doing?

MRS. MOODIE Miss Chandler, who is she?

SARAH	She's a woman who's made a mistake!
MARIA	I did not!
SARAH	(*to MARIA*) Mrs. Wait, please...we're in public...

The PURSER enters.

PURSER	Ladies...
MARIA	(*at the same time*) I don't care!
PURSER	Ladies!
SARAH	Is there another cabin free?
PURSER	Just one female cabin on the *St. George*. Unless you want to tow your maids behind.
MARIA	I'm not her maid.
PURSER	Honest mistake, no need to get uppity. Hello, now you mention it, where did you come from?
PEGGY	She jumped...
PURSER	She best have five dollars or she can jump again.
MARIA	Five dollars! You're joking...
PURSER	Yes, ma'am. That's it. We built this ship and sail her just to play a joke on you.
SARAH	(*to MARIA*) I'm no longer in a position to assist you...I did some shopping yesterday — (*breaking off as she sees MARIA take money from her pocket*)
MARIA	When will we reach Kingston?
PURSER	I could say tomorrow noon, (*exiting*) but I might be lying.

MARIA	But I have to catch the stage!
MRS. MOODIE	Clearly, we all have to learn to be patient.
MARIA	Patient! My husband is going to be hanged and quartered in two weeks and you tell me —
MRS. MOODIE	God preserve us!
MARIA	— to be patient!
MRS. MOODIE	Can this creature be a rebel?
MARIA	A patriot's wife, madam. And that (*pointing to SARAH*) is a patriot's daughter.
MRS. MOODIE	Gather our bags, Peggy. (*exiting*) I'm not going to risk having our throats cut in the night.
SARAH	(*to MARIA*) Must you make things even more horrible than they are?
MARIA	What were you trying to do? Pass yourself off as a member of the gentry?
PEGGY	You Canadians don't know gentry from cabbages. Herself became a duchess when she left Liverpool. (*exiting with baggage*) She was nowt at home.

> *Silence. SARAH and MARIA stare at each other. Lights change to morning.*

Scene Three

A STREET CORNER IN TORONTO

MACDONALD enters.

MACDONALD	Monday, August thirteenth. (*taking out his watch, tapping it, and puts it back in his pocket*) Eight A.M. or close to it.

ROBINSON enters from another direction.

MACDONALD	Mr. Robinson...
ROBINSON	If you wish to see me, make an appointment at my office.
MACDONALD	Your secretary said you were busy.
ROBINSON	As I am, Mr. MacDonald.
MACDONALD	Sir! (*as ROBINSON exits*) Damn you.

MACDONALD exits in the other direction.

Scene Two continues...

ON THE *S.S. ST. GEORGE*

MARIA is waking up from an uncomfortable night sitting on the bench. SARAH is watching her. She has thought of a scheme and breaks the silence tentatively.

SARAH	Good morning, Mrs. Wait...(*as MARIA looks away from her*) You know, it's silly to spend another day in silence.
MARIA	I've nothing to say to you.
SARAH	But there really has been a misunderstanding. The young man you saw...
MARIA	Young Robinson.

SARAH

It may have been. I didn't know. I twisted my ankle going aboard...a gentleman helped me to a seat. I had no occasion to ask his name.

MARIA

Is that true?

SARAH

Of course it is...and I didn't mean to go off without you either. I thought you'd changed your mind.

MARIA

Where did you get an idea like that?

SARAH

I heard Mrs. Beemer tell you your child would die.

MARIA

Oh.

SARAH

You weren't there when the whistle blew...I assumed that...naturally...you'd decided that your baby came first.

MARIA

I couldn't let Ben hang, could I?

SARAH

Then...where is she?

MARIA

Mrs. Beemer and Lizzie are looking after her.

SARAH

But...how?

MARIA

They'll be giving her cow's milk.

SARAH

Oh, dear.

MARIA

All babies have to switch sometime, don't they? (*beat*) Don't they?

SARAH

(*with grave doubt*) I'm sure she'll be fine. Speaking quite selfishly, (*rising with a pronounced limp*) I'm delighted not to be alone. I gather Mrs. Beemer parted with some of the thousand dollars?

MARIA

Nonsense. She had a few pennies for the ferry...she had nothing more to give me except...

SARAH	Except..?
MARIA	My watch back. All right...She lied about selling it...but she only wanted to drive a better bargain later on.
SARAH	So...you sold it yourself?
MARIA	It took me all morning to find a pawnbroker who lived above his store. (*beat*) How did you manage to shop on a Sunday?
SARAH	A friend of mine knew a merchant who was kind enough to open.
MARIA	What friend?
SARAH	A woman...an older woman...the woman I stayed with Saturday night. Now, shall we celebrate the end of our quarrel by having breakfast together?
MARIA	I couldn't eat.
SARAH	Meals on this ship are included in the fare. On the smaller ones, and on the stage, we'll have to pay for food.
MARIA	(*rising*) I would never have thought of that.
SARAH	I haven't sold a gold watch...
MARIA	I have sufficient to last me if I'm careful, that's all.
SARAH	It's a shame you haven't some to send to Mrs. Beemer. (*exiting*) We can only pray she finds enough to pay for Augusta's milk.
MARIA	Miss Chandler...
SARAH	(*turning to her*) Oh, I'm sorry. I shouldn't add to your worries.

MARIA	Well, we needn't worry about your ankle, need we? I see it's completely healed.

They exit with bags as...

Scene Four

A STREET IN TORONTO

ROBINSON enters, pursued by MACDONALD.

MACDONALD	If you let me into your office, I wouldn't be forced to accost you on the street!
ROBINSON	(*to the audience*) Tuesday, August fourteenth. Add tenacity to this lad's initiative.
MACDONALD	Sir, how do you square misleading our hopes with your conscience?
ROBINSON	(*moving*) That's impertinent.
MACDONALD	You've been the epitome of honour throughout your career. Your personal integrity is a legend at our *Alma Mater*.
ROBINSON	(*surprised*) You attended my school?
MACDONALD	It was you who inspired me to become a lawyer.
ROBINSON	(*intrigued*) Yet you sympathize with Reform?

MACDONALD   I don't have to agree with a client in order to do my best for him. Besides, sir, you said it yourself, the rebels posed no threat to Upper Canada or anyone in it. So why not advise the Governor to commute the sentence and avoid a blot on your reputation?

ROBINSON   (*laughing*) You're good, MacDonald. You have a future in front of you.

MACDONALD   There's an even better reason for commutation....there's a rumour Lord Durham's granted amnesty in Quebec.

ROBINSON   Yes, His Lordship mentioned that during his all too brief state visit...but the Governor of Quebec does not dictate policy here.

MACDONALD   Sir, we can't have two standards of justice in the country.

ROBINSON   We don't have a country yet. We have two equal but separate colonies.

MACDONALD   Are you hanging three men over a question of jurisdiction?

ROBINSON   The question is one of sovereignty.

MACDONALD   The bug bear of Quebec domination...is that what you're afraid of?

ROBINSON   That, and a great deal more.

MACDONALD   (*light dawning*) You're trying to keep us clear of the Durham report! You're afraid of what Radical Jack might recommend!

ROBINSON   I know what he'll recommend. Mobocracy...the American curse on the civilized world. I shed blood on Queenston Heights, before you were born, to save this colony from that catastrophe. I'll execute as many rebels as it takes to keep it that way.

MACDONALD	Then Sam Chandler has no hope at all?
ROBINSON	MacDonald, it's time to cut your losses and move on.
MACDONALD	I'm sorry to hear that, sir...(*heeding ROBINSON's advice*) but I suppose a man in your position sometimes has to choose the lesser evil.
ROBINSON	(*glad to be understood*) Hard decisions are the price of office.

LUKIN enters.

LUKIN	Father, I was on my way to see you.
ROBINSON	What is it you want?
LUKIN	(*looking at MACDONALD*) It's a private matter.
ROBINSON	Private matters can wait till I'm at home. (*turning his back on LUKIN, taking MACDONALD's arm and leading him aside*) You, my boy, have the good sense this county is going to need.If you're interested, I have an opening on my staff?
LUKIN	Father...
MACDONALD	(*beat*) Sir...that's a bolt from the blue...
LUKIN	I say, Father...
MACDONALD	May I have a few days to think it over?
ROBINSON	Think about this, MacDonald. How do wish to spend your life? As a county lawyer with a clear conscience, or a statesmen with the power to decide the course of history?

MACDONALD bows slightly, and exits.

LUKIN	Actually, I've decided I'd like to keep my job.

ROBINSON	Why the change of heart?
LUKIN	Well...to tell you the truth...I'm completely flat.
ROBINSON	(*more in sorrow than anger*) Lukin...it would have been better for you if I had let the rebels win.

> *ROBINSON exits. LUKIN follows him.*

Scene Five

THE PIER AT LONG SAULT

> *The benches used in the boat scene may be inverted to represent a pier. SARAH and MARIA enter carrying their bags. MARIA plunks hers down. SARAH sits, still clasping hers.*

MARIA	You can put down your bag. No one's here to steal it.

> *MARIA paces impatiently.*

SARAH	(*to the audience*) We're waiting for the stagecoach at Long Sault. How do I get rid of this woman! I can think of no lie that wouldn't lead her to the truth with two or three questions. Why am I afraid to tell her the truth? Oh, dear God. Why am I the oldest sister? Why is so much depending on *me*?
MARIA	I wish you'd stop sighing, Miss Chandler.
SARAH	I was imagining how awful this journey is for you. You couldn't have had time to say good-bye to your husband.

MARIA	You didn't say good-bye to your father either.
SARAH	My mother can visit Papa. Poor Mr. Wait has no one else, does he? (*no response*) And if we're delayed, or if Lord Durham refuses, he'll die without ever seeing you again.
MARIA	What choice do I have!
SARAH	And you must be worried about Augusta too. I had a baby sister who became very ill on cow's milk.
MARIA	Are you trying to drive me mad?
SARAH	I feel so guilty. If I'd been thinking back at Niagara, I'd have found a way to leave word...to let you know that I'd appeal for Mr. Wait too.
MARIA	Would you?
SARAH	Of course.
MARIA	Even though you think I'm a horrible woman?
SARAH	I know better now...I know you were right about the Chief Justice.
MARIA	Well...you were right about the jury.
SARAH	I've learned to listen to you since then, and I'm more sensible than you thought, aren't I?
MARIA	I suppose...
SARAH	Then, why don't you go back? Save your baby, and rely on me to save your husband?
MARIA	(*doubtful*) It's good of you to offer...
SARAH	You can take the boat back to Kingston, catch the steamship to Toronto...you'll be in Niagara with your baby at your breast in no time.

MARIA	But Ben...how can I leave his life in anyone else's hands...and what about poor Jake? Are you willing to plead for him too?
SARAH	(*taken aback*) Well...
MARIA	Mrs. Beemer didn't think you would. That's why she gave me my watch.
SARAH	All right...listen...you're good at letters, aren't you? Why don't you write out your appeal and let me deliver it?
MARIA	That's an idea...
SARAH	I brought stationary.

> *SARAH rummages in her bag. MARIA comes close. SARAH manoeuvers the bag away from her.*

MARIA	It's just...if you don't get to see him, I'd never forgive myself.
SARAH	(*passing her stationary*) Here you are. Oh, I'm going to see him. I've made certain of that.
MARIA	But I don't know how do to address an Earl? Is it...Excellency or what?
SARAH	(*finding her magazine*) Look in *The Albion*.. All his titles are listed.
MARIA	(*taking it*) Thank you.
SARAH	(*continuing to rummage*) Here's a pen...and ink...and...(*making a makeshift desk from Maria's bag*) This will give you a surface of sorts...
MARIA	(*reading*) Miss Chandler!
SARAH	What is it?

MARIA	His Commission. I had no idea how much power he has!
SARAH	I told you he's the Queen's cousin.
MARIA	That and how pretty he looked! It says here that he advocated the secret ballot six years ago.
SARAH	(*not interested*) Did he?
MARIA	He helped to get the Reform Bill passed in England!
SARAH	You'd best hurry...I think I hear the boat...
MARIA	Don't you understand? The Earl of Durham is on my side! He can do more than save Ben and your father. He can save our country!
SARAH	(*realizing her plot is in danger*) You could write about that too.
MARIA	You don't even care, do you?
SARAH	(*flaring*) I care about people, Mrs. Wait, I care about my family and your baby.
MARIA	But not about their liberty?
SARAH	Oh, fiddlesticks.
MARIA	I beg your pardon?
SARAH	We weren't slaves or anything, were we? We were happy.
MARIA	Maybe you were!
SARAH	Anybody could have been, if they didn't get mixed up in stupid politics!
MARIA	Is that what you're going to say to Lord Durham, spare the prisoners because they were stupid?

SARAH   All I intend to do is beg for mercy.

MARIA   Well, I intend to demand justice, Miss Chandler.
               And a parliament responsible to the people.

SARAH   For God's sake, what comfort is a parliament
               responsible to the people going to be if your
               husband and child are dead?

               *They stare at each other in silence, then
               MARIA walks to the other side of the
               stage.*

MARIA   I no longer speak to Sarah Chandler. She no
               longer speaks to me. But the question still
               speaks. It echoes on all the land and water we
               cross from Long Sault to Sorrel. And there's
               another echo...Ben's words..."Maybe she loves
               him enough not to care about defeats or
               victories." Could he have been happy if we'd
               turned our backs on the fight? Every time I close
               my eyes I see my baby reaching for me. But
               what future would be hers if her father hangs? If
               her country remains in chains?

Scene Six

A PIER ON THE RIVER, MONTREAL, LOWER CANADA

               *A PORTER enters and repositions one
               bench to make a different pier..*

PORTER   Mercredi, Le quinzieme août, Montréal. Le
               bateau arrive...cinq...(*holding up five fingers*)
               minutes...(*reaching for the bags*) S'il vous plait.

SARAH   No! Don't touch that! No! (*snatching her bag*)

MARIA	(*to the audience*) What does she have in there? The Crown jewels?
PORTER	(*exiting*) Maudites Anglaise.
SARAH	(*crossing to MARIA*) We'll be in Quebec City tomorrow, Mrs. Wait. Shouldn't we lay aside our quarrel and discuss our plans?
MARIA	What plans?
SARAH	I think it would be best if I saw the Earl first.
MARIA	Why?
SARAH	Nothing I'm likely to say will prejudice your case, but if you go in there and start ranting, I'll —
MARIA	Ranting!
SARAH	— never be allowed near him!
MARIA	I intend to see Lord Durham the first moment I possibly can. I only pray there's ivy near his window.
SARAH	Ivy!
MARIA	So I can climb up!
SARAH	Is that what you intend to do? Break into the Castle St. Louis?
MARIA	If I have to. (*beat*) Miss Chandler...why were you so sure Lord Durham would see you?
SARAH	I'm not...
MARIA	You were yesterday...when you were trying to make me go back.
SARAH	I was trying to do you a favour.

MARIA	I don't believe you. You've something up your sleeve. No, not your sleeve...

MARIA picks up SARAH's bag.

SARAH	Mrs. Wait...that's mine...(*MARIA opens SARAH's bag and finds a letter*) Don't you touch that!
MARIA	(*holding it away from her*) The seal of the Chief Justice! How did you get a letter from him!
SARAH	(*clawing after the letter*) Give it to me!
MARIA	(*grabbing her*) You little devil! You're a Tory spy!

MARIA gets a firm hold on SARAH.

SARAH	No, no...please.
MARIA	You tell me the truth or —

MARIA propels her to the edge of the pier.

SARAH	Let go of me!
MARIA	I'll throw you in the river —
SARAH	No!
MARIA	I mean it! I'll drown you!
SARAH	All right! Lukin Robinson wrote it.
MARIA	(*letting go*) Then you did know him?
SARAH	He let me use his father's seal.
MARIA	Why? What did you do for him?
SARAH	Nothing.

MARIA   Liar! No Robinson would do something for nothing. (*grabbing SARAH again*) What did you do for him? Tell me or I'll push you off!

SARAH   What do you think I did?

MARIA   (*releasing SARAH, a pause*) Oh, Miss Chandler...(*silence*) Oh, my dear, your father would never have wanted that.

SARAH   I didn't do it for my father.

MARIA   What?

SARAH   My father abandoned us. Some ratty little stranger came knocking at our door and he never spared us a thought. We could all end up starving because of him. I did what I had to keep my family's property! If it weren't for that, I'd let my father hang.

MARIA   Then you are a proper little trollop!

SARAH   But I'm not a traitor! The jailer found that letter you smuggled to your husband.

MARIA   No...

SARAH   Mr. Robinson read it, and Governor Arthur read it.

MARIA   I don't believe you! It's another of your lies.

SARAH   I lied because I had pity on you. I didn't want you to know that your letter is the reason they sentenced your husband to die.

MARIA   No...

SARAH   It wasn't because he refused to confess. It wasn't what he said at his trial! He was singled out because of your treason!

MARIA   Oh God, no!

SARAH   And that's not all, Mrs. Wait. Lord Durham has read that letter too! (*beat*) Now do you understand why I left you in Niagara? Why I tried to make you go back? Can you get it through your head that my father and your husband have no chance at all unless you let me see Durham alone! (*silence, stretching out her hand*) May I have my letter of introduction, please?

                MARIA hands it to her. They walk to
                opposite sides of the stage.

MARIA   (*to the audience*) It's clear to me now. Clear and cold as the river. This is why I came on this journey. This is why I refused to go back. It's not because I had a hope of saving Ben. It's because I'm too much of a coward to stand underneath the gallows, knowing it's my fault he's there.

                MARIA leaves the stage. SARAH
                watches her go. The pier is struck.

Scene Seven

AN ANTEROOM IN THE CASTLE ST. LOUIS,
QUEBEC, LOWER CANADA

                A FOOTMAN enters. SARAH crosses to
                him, hands him her letter.

SARAH   (*to the audience*) I spend all of Thursday standing in an anteroom at Lord Durham's residence. Finally I am told to return tomorrow.

> *The FOOTMAN places a chair and a small
> table with a drawer - preset with paper,
> pen, sealing wax, candle - in one corner of
> the stage for SARAH. He exits.*

SARAH At least today, I've been invited to sit.

Scene Eight

A CORRIDOR IN THE CASTLE

> *SARAH sits as DURHAM enters another
> area of the stage in his dressing gown, and
> carrying papers. He is pursued by
> COLONEL COUPER.*

COUPER My lord, what do you think you're doing!

DURHAM (*looking up from his papers*) Oh, Coups. I'm
trying to create a country on paper. It's rather like
putting a picture puzzle together. Except there is
no picture...just these little pieces of briefs...the
ones from French nationalists, the ones from
Upper Canadian Loyalists...all square edged...all
without any spaces to let the others fit in.

COUPER Damn them, Sir, you must go back to bed.

DURHAM Damn them...yet her darling little Majesty tells
me I am responsible for their immortal souls?

COUPER I'm not sure colonials have souls.

DURHAM The darling little Prime Minister tells me I am
responsible for the ship-building trade.

COUPER If people stayed where they belonged, we
wouldn't need ships.

DURHAM   It's too late to think of that. The people are here. (*looking at paper*) What kind of a country do they want me to piece together for them?

COUPER   To bed, sir...please...

DURHAM   And does it matter what I do? Will the Americans have it anyway? Mr. Robinson says they covet all the new world. That's rather mean of them, since God gave this part of it to Victoria for the relief of England's poor. I know because she told me so. I don't know who told her. Either God or the Prime Minister.

COUPER   My lord...

DURHAM   It must have been God. The poor don't vote, you see. But I've heard they pray a good deal.

COUPER   How much laudanum have you taken this morning?

DURHAM   Coups, are we to be invaded, yeah or nay?

COUPER   Colonial intelligence has turned up, please don't shout at me, virtually nothing.

DURHAM   (*shouting*) Colonial intelligence is a —

COUPER   A contradiction in terms, yes, sir. Nevertheless, they do have word of a few individuals calling themselves the William Lyon Mackenzie Association, dedicated to fomenting revolt from the safe side of the border...so Mr. Robinson's American agent wasn't entirely off his rocker.

DURHAM   *Her* rocker. How could you forget? Is there a link between republicanism and eroticism, Coups?

COUPER   Not judging by the American women I've seen.

>*A FOOTMAN enters with a tray, on which are calling cards and a new copy of* The Albion. *COUPER takes the tray from him. The FOOTMAN exits.*

DURHAM   I've often fancied myself in dear Ben's nightcap. I wonder what she looks like? [*change adjectives to be opposite of the actress playing MARIA*] Blonde and delicate, I imagine. (*sifting through the cards on the tray*) Mr. Simpson, Bishop Mountain...Miss Sarah Chandler. Who is Miss Sarah Chandler?

COUPER   A young person, sir. I brought up her letter of introduction yesterday.

DURHAM   (*bored*) Oh, yes, Mr. Robinson's sad case of utmost respectability.

COUPER   (*picking up the magazine from the footman's tray*) Now here's a copy of this week's *Albion*, still in its wrapper. You can relax with the juicy gossip those carrier pigeons brought you from London.

DURHAM   (*taking it*) You don't care if I lose the Canadas, do you, Coups?

COUPER   As long we don't lose you, sir.

DURHAM   You're going to do that anyway. And ruining a nice new nation is not the sort of accomplishment I want listed in my obituary.

COUPER   Stop your nonsense. You'll live for years if you take care of yourself. Now come along.

>*COUPER and FOOTMAN lead DURHAM off as...*

Scene Nine

THE ANTEROOM

> *The FOOTMAN enters. SARAH springs*
> *to her feet.*

FOOTMAN

An urgent message brought by (*as MARIA
enters*) your maid, miss. (*exits*)

SARAH

(*after the FOOTMAN*) No, you've made a
mistake!

MARIA

They will inscribe those words on your
tombstone, Miss Chandler.

SARAH

Get out of here! Go!

MARIA

Your introduction didn't carry you far. I guess it
wasn't worth the price —

SARAH

Mrs. Wait...

MARIA

— cheap though it may have been.

SARAH

Please, you'll have us both thrown out!

MARIA

I'm not going to rant. I won't even mention
politics. I'll say what I have to, and face the
consequence. That's all.

> *COUPER enters, followed by the*
> *FOOTMAN. He looks at MARIA, then*
> *ignores her.*

COUPER

(*to SARAH*) I'm sorry, it's another migraine.
Perhaps if you call again tomorrow.

SARAH

Colonel, I was hoping to catch the boat at noon.

COUPER:

Surely you can take the next one, can't you?

MARIA	Yes, Colonel, she can take any number of next boats, but her father will be dead by the time she reaches Niagara.
COUPER	(*amazed that she speaks*) Is this your servant, Miss Chandler?
	SARAH shakes her head, as MARIA plows on.
MARIA	Sir, it has taken us five days to reach Quebec. We have waited here two days. There is no more time. Lord Durham must see us now.
COUPER	Lord Durham must?
MARIA	Pardon me. I don't know the etiquette for such occasions. How is a widow-to-be supposed to behave?
COUPER	My good woman!
MARIA	If we do not have an answer, I will return to find my husband hanged and quartered. It will be beyond the power of even the Queen's cousin to breathe life back into him.
SARAH	Sir, all I ask is one small moment.
COUPER	I'm sorry. (*beckoning the FOOTMAN to usher them out*) Be good little lambs now...
MARIA	(*crossing to the chair and sitting*) I will remain here until Lord Durham is well enough to receive me.
COUPER	Not permitted, madam.
DURHAM	(*off, shouting*) Coups!
MARIA	Three men shouldn't die because of a headache, sir —
DURHAM	(*off, shouting over MARIA's line*) Coups!

MARIA	— no matter whose head it is!
	DURHAM crashes into the scene in time to hear the last. He is waving The Albion.
COUPER	My lord!
DURHAM	(*turning to MARIA*) Who the devil are you?
MARIA	I have the honour to be Mrs. Benjamin Wait.
DURHAM	Your loving Maria? Truly? Is this you?
SARAH	(*curtseying*) Your Lordship...
COUPER	(*indicating SARAH*) My lord, may I present —
DURHAM	No, no, I'm not presentable. (*to MARIA*) How is dearest Ben?
MARIA	In prison, about to be hanged...my...lordship.
DURHAM	My lord, your lordship. Simple when you get the - hanged, you say?
SARAH	My lord, we've come to beg for mercy.
MARIA	For justice. If you are just, you'll send me to the gallows and let my husband go.
DURHAM	Quite right. You must never, never, never, refer to the Queen as a slip of a girl. That is treason.
MARIA	I'm the guilty —
DURHAM	(*over her*) She is very tiny, but it is treason all the same.
MARIA	Ben didn't —
DURHAM	(*over her*) And you must never, never, never say you don't want to be ruled by her. That's not fair. She's just started you know, and she did promise to be good.

SARAH	My lord, please..
DURHAM	(*to MARIA, pointing at SARAH*) She's about her age, and she says please in just that tone. I wouldn't be here if she didn't. (*tossing the magazine on the table*) Maria, are the Americans going to invade us?
MARIA	I don't think so.
DURHAM	Try to keep the regret out of your voice, as a courtesy while you're in my presence. How many members are there in the William Lyon Mackenzie association?
MARIA	I...I don't know.
DURHAM	You wrote there was an army?
MARIA	I was exaggerating.
DURHAM	To what purpose?
MARIA	I was trying to give my husband hope.
DURHAM	Yes, of course. (*to COUPER*) Whether it's execution or consumption, everyone wants to give hope when there is none.
MARIA	There is, sir, there must be...my lord.
DURHAM	Sir will do. Hope for what, Maria?
MARIA	For my husband. He only received my letter. It was I who wrote those things...
DURHAM	You also wrote your dreams would soon come true?
MARIA	(*hesitating*) I was being foolish...
DURHAM	What did you dream of?
MARIA	(*hesitating*) Oh...what everybody dreams of...

DURHAM	But what...specifically?
MARIA	(*trying to come up with something harmless*) A family.
DURHAM	Is that all?
MARIA	(*not a good liar*) A home. A peaceful life.
DURHAM	Maria, is that all?
SARAH	(*quickly*) Yes, my lord, that's all.
DURHAM	(*turning to her*) Do you have a husband too?
SARAH	A father, sir.
DURHAM	Which was he? One of the misled hooligans, the thief, or perhaps the raving lunatic?
SARAH	(*a pause*) The lunatic.
MARIA	(*flaring up*) If Sam Chandler is a lunatic, then, by God, so are you!
COUPER	Madam!
SARAH	(*at the same time*) Mrs. Wait!
MARIA	Both her father and my husband fought for the same things you fought for in England.
DURHAM	(*surprised*) You know what I fought for?
MARIA	You stopped patronage in Parliament. We don't have a parliament, but we sure have patronage!
DURHAM	(*pleased*) Go on.
MARIA	The secret ballot! We don't have it either, so men are beaten up, sometimes murdered. People are terrified into Toryism!
DURHAM	What a lovely phrase, and so apt.

SARAH	Sir, please...
DURHAM	(*ignoring her*) Maria, if you had a parliament, what would you do?
MARIA	Not me, sir. The people. We'd put this country to use!
DURHAM	How? Tell me how?
MARIA	First of all...we'd stop The Family Compact from granting all the land to themselves.
DURHAM	Family Compact?
MARIA	John Robinson and his clique.
DURHAM	Another lovely phrase. What else?
MARIA	Well...as it is now, you have to borrow money from their bank to start a farm, but one crop failure and...
DURHAM	The farmer loses his farm.
MARIA	He may have spent years chopping trees and picking stones...
DURHAM	The farmer loses his labour..
MARIA	And the bank sells cleared land at a higher price.
DURHAM	Thus wealth is accumulated.
MARIA	In the pockets of the few! While poverty and desperation are left to the rest of us. Sir, this country has land to grow food, trees to build homes, and room for millions to live in peace and plenty. All we want is the right to hold our heads up in a country that belongs to every person in it. And we could have it, sir. If people just used their common sense!

DURHAM   Oh, Maria, that isn't common sense...that's a
            Utopian fantasy.

MARIA   (*deflated*) But...why...why is it —

SARAH   (*finally getting a word in*) What does it matter?
            My father's life is what matters. (*to MARIA*)
            And your husband's, remember!

MARIA   (*to DURHAM*) She's right...their lives...theirs
            and Jake Beemer's.

DURHAM   Is there a third condemned?

MARIA   Yes, sir.

DURHAM   Then...is he the thief?

MARIA   He's a poor woman's son. She crossed the ocean
            because she hoped he'd have a better life. Sir, I
            love my husband, I want him to live and I don't
            mean to rant at you...but you're wrong. Men
            with position and wealth always call our hopes a
            fantasy...as if only tyranny and greed were real!
            Our hope of liberty and justice is common
            sense...it's Robinson's hopes that should be the
            fantasy. He thinks he can pitchfork himself into
            power without anyone's leave. He and his kind
            want to create a new aristocracy...more viscous
            and arrogant than the one we left behind. They'll
            turn out to be greater scourge on this country
            than those useless parasites, the kings and —

COUPER   Don't say it!

            Silence.

SARAH   (*hushed*) Oh, God.

DURHAM   Madam, you go too far.

            *COUPER signals the FOOTMAN who
            takes a step forward.*

MARIA	Oh...I'm sorry...I didn't mean you...
SARAH	My lord, I beg you...
	The FOOTMAN places a hand on MARIA'S arm, SARAH faints gracefully at DURHAM's feet.
MARIA	Miss Chandler!
COUPER	(*to FOOTMAN*) Brandy and water.
	COUPER picks her up and deposits her in the chair.
DURHAM	(*to COUPER*) Isn't she a pretty little thing?
COUPER	And no republican, not a bit of it.
DURHAM	Indeed not. Republicans aren't as accomplished in the drawing room arts.
MARIA	Is she all right?
DURHAM	(*to MARIA*) What a clever child she is to give us pause. You and I have time to lay down our weapons before more blood is spilled.
MARIA	My lord, there was never bloodshed on our side.
DURHAM	Oh, but there will be. That's what we few with power don't understand. We might have snuffed out your passion with a little generosity. We never learn that repression only guarantees bloodier outbreaks, which we will meet with bloodier repression again and again. Ideas of liberty are like the falls of Niagara, they will not be stopped by borders. And if we are fools enough to try to dam them, there will one day come such a flood, such a deluge that all the useless aristocrats and all the rebellious Maria's, all dreams and all reason will be swept away.
MARIA	Sir, if you understand that, you could save us.

DURHAM	I wish I could.
SARAH	(*rising*) My lord, all we're asking is a pardon.
DURHAM	(*to SARAH*) You may be asking for a pardon. (*pointing to MARIA*) She's asking for a new world. A world where common sense prevails. I cannot give it to her. I am going home.
MARIA	But your report?
DURHAM	There'll be a dispatch on the ship, the one that brought the pigeon that brought the news to *The Albion*. That dispatch says the Durham Report is never to be written.
COUPER	(*grabbing up the magazine*) Bloody hell.
DURHAM	I am recalled. And you know why? Because I employed my common sense, because I granted mercy in Lower Canada without due process of law. Butchery is within the law, you see, but mercy might cause the British Empire to tumble down.
SARAH	Then we've come all this way for nothing?
DURHAM	Yes, my dear, and so have I.
MARIA	I don't understand...the ship hasn't come yet?
DURHAM	I am dating my resignation as of this moment. I will not give my enemies the satisfaction of bringing about my fall.
COUPER	(*taking DURHAM's arm*) Let me take you to your room.
MARIA	No! My lord, if you turn your back on Ben and Mr. Chandler and Jake Beemer when you still have time to save them, then I was right. You are a useless aristocrat! And a parasite!
COUPER	For God's sake, can't you see how ill he is!

DURHAM   Never mind, Coups. She will only say three men should not die because a useless aristocrat is ill. (*indicating table*) That will serve me, Coups.

COUPER   (*to the FOOTMAN*) Fetch His Lordship's seal.

FOOTMAN exits. COUPER resets the table if necessary, and takes the writing materials from the table drawer and sets them up for DURHAM's use. MARIA crosses to SARAH.

SARAH   Oh, bless you, sir.

COUPER lights a candle to melt the wax. The FOOTMAN brings the seal.

COUPER   May be a futile exercise. Arthur will have read *The Albion* too.

DURHAM   (*to COUPER*) I imagine he's been hoping for my recall. Perhaps for that reason he'll forego belief till the dispatch is in his hands. (*sitting and writing as he speaks*) Even so, I daren't issue a pardon. I will merely entreat my fellow governor to return your loved ones to you...I'll couch it in such terms, he'll find no reason to dig in his heels again. (*sealing his note*) My last official act. The last word I shall write on behalf of the Canadas. Hardly the sort of thing to be remembered.

DURHAM rises and hands the note to MARIA.

SARAH   I'll remember, my lord.

DURHAM   (*to COUPER*) Coups, order the staff to pack up. We sail for England at the first possible moment.

MARIA   Are you truly going to sail away and leave this country in the hands of the few?

DURHAM	Dear loving Maria...(*a pause*) How I wish I had met you while I was young.

DURHAM exits.

COUPER	When is the date for executions?
MARIA	A week from tomorrow.
COUPER	You'll have to travel like the wind. And pray very hard that the real dispatch doesn't.
MARIA	We shall, my lord.
SARAH	Maria...our boat...we still have time to catch it.

MARIA and SARAH run off. COUPER and FOOTMAN take table and chair off as...

Scene Ten

THE GARDEN of BEVERLEY HOUSE, TORONTO

LUKIN enters in fancy dress. He has a drink, not his first, in his hand.

LUKIN	(*to the audience*) Friday, August twenty fourth. The theme of our ball is Conquering Heroes.

ROBINSON and MACDONALD enter.

MACDONALD	I checked before I left the office...there's still nothing from England.

LUKIN steps toward them.

ROBINSON	(*ignoring LUKIN*) Perhaps the ship hit a storm.

MACDONALD   There's no word from Quebec either.

ROBINSON   Durham's hardly going to notify Arthur of his humiliation.

MACDONALD   I meant about tomorrow's executions. (*ostentatiously checking MARIA's gold watch*) There's only sixteen hours to go.

ROBINSON   I see you spent your first wages, my boy.

MACDONALD   As a matter of fact, it was quite a bargain...I found it at a pawnbroker's.

ROBINSON   Lukin, fetch us some drinks, will you?

LUKIN   Don't we have servants, father?

ROBINSON   Your mother has them occupied, while you, as usual, are standing idle.

EMMA enters in costume and domino, carrying a bag large enough for another costume.

EMMA   Is this the young man who's going to oblige us?

ROBINSON   Oh, yes...Emma, you haven't met my new assistant.

EMMA   I hear you're named John, too? That must be confusing to your staff.

MACDONALD   Your husband has become John B. around the office, Mrs. Robinson. I'm now known as John A.

MERRITT enters, The Albion *in hand.*

MERRITT   John, I just got in from Welland and found *The Albion.* I suppose that's the end of Quebec stealing our prosperity?

EMMA   If the story is true, Mr. Merritt.

MERRITT   You think it isn't?

ROBINSON   I'd say your investments were safe.

                *LUKIN arrives with drinks. ROBINSON
                and MERRITT take one.*

MERRITT   Then, by God, let's start the celebration.

MACDONALD   I don't drink, thank you. (*to MERRITT, as
                LUKIN sets down the tray with drink meant for
                MACDONALD*) You must be the Mr. Merritt of
                the Welland Canal?

MERRITT   Are you interested in transportation, yourself?

MACDONALD   If this province is to realize its potential, we need
                access to the resources of the west.

MERRITT   What do you mean, province?

EMMA   (*passing MACDONALD the bag*) Before you get
                into a discussion, John A., you must put on
                your costume. Lukin will show you where you
                can change.

LUKIN   (*exiting with MACDONALD*) Would you care to
                take my bedroom, Mr. MacDonald? Since you
                already have my job.

ROBINSON   Do you have a son, Mr. Merritt?

MERRITT   I've not been blessed, no.

ROBINSON   Perhaps you've been more blessed than you
                imagine.

                They exit as...

Scene Eleven

A DECK ON YET ANOTHER BOAT

> *MARIA and SARAH enter, exhausted, but in high spirits.*

MARIA	There it is! Toronto harbour!
SARAH	(*hugging her*) Maria...we've made it.
MARIA	Government House isn't far from the dock.
SARAH	If all goes well, we can catch the late ferry.
MARIA	I can't wait to hold Augusta.
SARAH	I don't want Papa to think tonight is his last on earth.
MARIA	I thought you hated your father?
SARAH	Oh, well...I may never understand why he did what he did, but I'm not as mad at him...now that everything's turned out all right.
MARIA	Sarah, everything hasn't turned out all right yet.
SARAH	We're sure of a pardon, aren't we?
MARIA	We still have Arthur and Robinson to contend with. Because Durham doesn't have the courage of his convictions!
SARAH	You are the most ungrateful woman alive.
MARIA	I suppose you're grateful to everyone, aren't you? Even to young Robinson for making a whore out of you?
SARAH	Don't you ever say that again!

MARIA	When are you going to understand? It's people like you who make those bastards as powerful as they are.
SARAH	(*beat*) Maria, when we see the Governor, you must let me do the talking.
MARIA	Why? I did fine with Durham.
SARAH	You'd be in prison if I hadn't fainted. Besides, look at you! You couldn't blame anyone for taking you for my maid now.
MARIA	That woman on the boat wouldn't mistake you for gentry either.
SARAH	(*remembering*) Mrs. Moodie! She was going to miss the party - Maria, the Governor will be at Robinson's tonight.
MARIA	We have to find out where the house is.
SARAH	I've been there!
MARIA	(*delighted*) You have? Then I'll bet you know the back way in!

> *MARIA starts off as a SAILOR enters.*

SAILOR	Wait for the gangplank, eh? There's fifteen feet of water there.
SARAH	That's all right. She can stand on her tongue.

> *Scene Ten continues...*

> *They exit as ROBINSON enters pursued by EMMA. LUKIN drifts behind them. Music comes from offstage.*

EMMA	What is the point of my insisting our guests wear masks if you keep introducing them to each other?

ROBINSON   None at all, my dear.

MACNAB   (*off, from the street*) Piss on these bloody masks.

ROBINSON   You wouldn't want our most important guests to pass unrecognized, would you?

> *The MACNABS enter, he as Julius Caesar, she as Cleopatra.*

EMMA   Ah...it's Caesar and Calpurnia.

LADY MACNAB Cleopatra, Mrs. Robinson. Lady Cleopatra.

MACNAB   I know I said I wanted to be in society, Johnny, but are you making a fool of me?

EMMA   (*as she leads LADY MACNAB off into the house*) Ladies and Gentlemen, our own Canadian conquering hero...

> *Applause off.*

MACNAB   Oh, piss. (*scurrying off*)

LUKIN   Time to go and pull some strings, father. Your brand new puppet is coming up the walk.

ROBINSON   Stay away from him, you've been drinking too much.

> *ARTHUR enters, from the street in Governor's regalia, not masked.*

ROBINSON   Sir George, everyone is talking about your victory.

ARTHUR   Can we put so much faith in pigeons?

> *EMMA enters. LADY MACNAB, MERRITT follow. Bagpipes or fiddles begin off.*

EMMA

(*curtseying*) Your Excellency, we've prepared a little entertainment to welcome you.

> *The PIPER or FIDDLER appears. In front is MACNAB holding a rope which ends in a noose around the neck of MACDONALD, who is dressed as Mackenzie, in a red fright wig. MACDONALD is singing to the tune of "Pop Goes the Weasel" and dancing a jig. Unnoticed, MARIA and SARAH enter.*

MACDONALD

"I tell a tale of little Mac
To end his life of evil
There's but one step for Mac to take
From the gallows to the devil."

ARTHUR

(*laughing, over the performance*) He dances well enough, but who on earth is the costume supposed to represent?

ROBINSON

Why, Mackenzie, sir. He always wore a red wig.

ARTHUR

Very clever.

> *MARIA steps forward and rips off the wig.*

ARTHUR

And who's the ragamuffin who just ripped it off?

MARIA

(*to MACDONALD*) You masquerade as a better man than you are.

> *The music stops, everyone reacts. LUKIN puts down his drink.*

EMMA

Is this someone's idea of humour?

MACDONALD

They're relatives of the condemned.

SARAH

(*to ARTHUR*) We hope His Excellency will pardon our temerity. (*curtsey, holding the letter toward him*) Please be kind enough to read what the Earl of Durham has written on our behalf.

ROBINSON	(*to ARTHUR*) Don't touch it, sir.
ARTHUR	As sole representative of the Queen in this colony, I decline to accept instruction from the Governor of Quebec.
MARIA	You won't even open it?
MACDONALD	Miss Chandler, you've mistaken the lines of authority. Come with me and —
LUKIN	Don't listen to him!
ROBINSON	Keep quiet!
MACNAB	You need some help here, Johnny?
SARAH	(*recognizing him*) Colonel MacNab...Oh, thank God.
MACNAB	(*to ROBINSON*) You want me to put them out?
EMMA	(*putting a restraining hand on MACNAB's arm*) No violence, no...
SARAH	Colonel...don't you recognize me? I'm Sarah Chandler. (*as EMMA looks at LUKIN*) I was your daughter's best friend...(*tearing the letter open and holding it out*) Please...read this! Tell the Governor he must read it! (*silence*) Please, Mrs. MacNab, look at it! (*silence*) What's wrong with you? You were my father's neighbours all your lives! Look! The Earl has spared his life!
	MACNAB takes the letter from her, and throws it on the ground. The others are shocked.
ROBINSON	You have your answer.
MARIA	Sarah...it's hopeless.
SARAH	Won't any of you speak for me? (*as others draw back*)

MARIA   We'll get no help from them.

ROBINSON   I will ask you once more to leave my property.

SARAH.   (*to ROBINSON*) No! No, you owe me a pardon!
                     I made Papa sign that confession you wanted! I
                     let you pretend he was insane...

ARTHUR   What's this?

SARAH   I did everything you asked of me! I did everything
                     your son asked up there in his bed!

                     *Everyone reacts. SARAH collapses in
                     tears.*

ARTHUR   God save us!

EMMA   (*overlapping to LUKIN*) Go to your room!

ROBINSON   (*overlapping*) Lunacy must run in her blood.

EMMA   (*overlapping, to LUKIN*) Quick! Before she says
                     more.

                     LUKIN exits. MACNAB grabs SARAH.

MACNAB   Come on, you little slut!

MARIA   Don't hurt her! We'll leave! (*picking up the
                     letter*) But I'm going back to Lord Durham! I'll
                     show him how you treated his letter!

                     A general murmur of confusion.

ROBINSON   Go where you wish, Mrs. Wait.

EMMA   (*frightened*) John, you're not certain...

                     ROBINSON signals her to be quiet.

MERRITT   (*waving* The Albion) Is this true or isn't it?

MARIA   *The Albion*? (*pausing, looking around at their
                 reactions*) Is that why you're so smug? Well, I've
                 a surprise for you, Mr. Robinson. The real
                 dispatch came while we were there! (*another
                 pause, but it's clear to MARIA her ruse is
                 working*) He hasn't been recalled at all! (*a
                 murmur of reaction*) He's been given even more
                 power!

ROBINSON   She's lying!

ARTHUR   A girl like her! She wouldn't have the wit. (*to
                 MARIA*) Let me see the document.

MARIA   Gladly, sir.

                 *MARIA holds it toward ARTHUR and he
                 takes it.*

ROBINSON   Even if he's Governor General, you could still
                 stand firm.

ARTHUR   (*scanning*) Oh! (*to ROBINSON*) This isn't an
                 order. (*public address*) Lord Durham *implores* me,
                 as a purely personal favour, to grant a reprieve.
                 He will use his influence for...ah, that's a private
                 note. (*to ROBINSON, passing him the
                 document*) John, we may oblige the Earl, I think.

MACDONALD   Sir, a compromise...one execution can establish
                 sovereignty. There's still the thief!

MARIA   Oh, God...

SARAH   (*over her*) No! Lord Durham included Jake
                 Beemer too.

ARTHUR   I think it's best if I reprieve all three.

                 *SARAH and MARIA clutch each other's
                 hands.*

ROBINSON   (*loudly*) Well, ladies and gentlemen, this
                 particular entertainment is over.

EMMA   Let's have some music, shall we? (*as music
                strikes up, offering her arm*) Sir George...

                        *ARTHUR takes her arm, they exit
                        followed by the guests except
                        MACDONALD and ROBINSON.*

ROBINSON   (*to MARIA*) So, you've had the best of me, Mrs.
                Wait...

MARIA   Hardly, Mr. Robinson. You still control the
                country.

ROBINSON   Had you your way, your Yankee friends would
                control it. (*dismissive*) You got what you came
                for.

SARAH   Maria, we've nothing in writing.

MACDONALD   You have the Governor's word. His Excellency is
                a man of honour.

SARAH   No, Mr. MacDonald, he only wears the costume,
                like the rest of you.

                        SARAH and MARIA exit.

ROBINSON   (*looking at the document, bitterly*) "I will use
                my influence to assure your next appointment is
                India."

MACDONALD   Well, I can't say I'll be sorry to have my
                conscience spared these deaths.

ROBINSON   Spare me your sentimentality. The Durham
                Report will be a disaster.

MACDONALD   You know, John B., the trouble with your
                generation is that you give too much weight to the
                Durham's of this world. And you underestimate the
                people. Even if he recommends a parliament,
                Canadians will choose our sort of government.
                They'll always know which side of the bread is
                buttered.

ROBINSON   Not if those rebels go free. If word of their
triumph spreads, they'll become heroes. Your
generation will inherit a chaotic society where
any fool who fancies himself aggrieved can pick
up a gun with impunity.

MACDONALD   Everybody heard the Governor's promise. There's
nothing you can do.

ROBINSON   No? Come and watch me.

> *ROBINSON exits into the house.
> MACDONALD sees the untouched drink,
> picks it up and for the first time in his
> life, downs it, before he follows
> ROBINSON off.*

Scene Twelve

THE SQUARE AT NIAGARA

> *The bell begins to toll. The empty
> gallows is fully lit. There could be the
> muted sound of scripture reading off.
> MARIA, carrying the baby, and SARAH
> enter from opposite sides of the stage.
> MARIA stands with her back to SARAH,
> in the same positions they occupied before
> the HANGMAN entered at the play's start.*

SARAH   (*to the audience*) Saturday, August 25. All the
scheduled boats from Toronto to Niagara have
come and gone. There has been no reprieve.

> *SARAH turns to MARIA and we are back
> in the first scene of the Act One.*

MARIA   You were right, Sarah. The freest parliament in
         the world wouldn't comfort me now.

SARAH   Maria, you're not to blame.

MARIA   They condemned him because of my letter. You
         told me so yourself.

SARAH   They would never have found your letter...or
         even known about it...if I hadn't told them.

MARIA   (*an intake of breath*) You sold me out?

SARAH   Your husband's death won't be your fault. It will
         be mine.

         *MARIA turns her back on SARAH.
         ANNIE and LIZZIE enter. WHEELER
         leads on the three PRISONERS. BEN
         pauses briefly. MARIA hides her face. The
         PRISONERS mount the scaffold steps.
         The HANGMAN enters.*

LIZZIE   Look! He's the wretch with mouths to feed!

ANNIE   Child, it's time to say our prayers.

LIZZIE   But ain't he? Ain't he the same as last time.

         *ANNIE kneels and begins the Rosary.
         LIZZIE joins her. The HANGMAN stares
         at them.*

HANGMAN I ain't doing it...not no more.

WHEELER You want more money?

HANGMAN I'd rather starve.

         The HANGMAN runs off.

WHEELER Jesus Christ, I'm going to have to do it myself.

> *In the confusion, MARIA and SARAH and ANNIE try to reach BEN and SAM and JAKE.*

MARIA Ben, I'm sorry —

SARAH Papa!

BEN Maria, don't watch!

> *A MESSENGER brings a note to WHEELER.*

WHEELER Hold everything! (*ALL focus on WHEELER, who reads*) "The Governor of Upper Canada has granted the petition for the lives of the three convicted traitors..." (*ALL rejoice*) Hold on...Hold on...there's more. "It is His Excellency's pleasure that they be given the lesser penalty of transportation for the rest of their natural lives..." (*beat*) You're going to the penal colony in Van Dieman's Land.

ANNIE Where?

WHEELER I'm to put you immediately aboard the Government boat. It's waiting for you at the dock.

ANNIE Where did he say?

WHEELER I'd rather have hung if it was me. (*to GUARD*) Get'em moving.

SARAH Papa...

BEN Can't we say good-bye?

WHEELER Be quick about it.

LIZZIE (*to JAKE*) Where?

JAKE I think it's the other side of the earth.

> *ANNIE and JAKE hold each other, as do*
> *BEN and MARIA.*

SAM Sarah, I was afraid I was going to my grave without you ever knowing why.

SARAH Papa, I do know.

SAM No, lass, how could you? I took Mackenzie across the river, but I came back. I got as far as our lane when I saw a crowd out in front of Jim Comfort's house. Then I saw the flames go up. It was Allan MacNab's militia, Sarah, men I knew, and Jim Comfort had known all his life. But MacNab told them that Comfort was the one that helped Mackenzie, and not one of those men had the courage to say no. That's when I turned around, Sarah...because it could have been my family they were burning out.

SARAH I understand...I understand now.

WHEELER Move them off!

MARIA Not yet...please, not yet! Ben...I don't know what to do next. I don't know where to turn.

BEN I'll get back, Maria. I'll swim if I have to.

WHEELER You women! Get off them!

Scene Thirteen

THE BOARDING HOUSE

> *The MEN move off. The WOMEN walk*
> *to the boarding house. No set is needed.*

ANNIE   I still can't take it in...Where did he say they
                   were sending them?

MARIA   It's near Australia, Annie.

LIZZIE   The other side of the earth.

ANNIE   Sure didn't I take him half way round?

SARAH   At least they're alive!

MARIA   If slavery is living.

                   *The baby is fussing in her arms, she
                   passes her to LIZZIE who handles her
                   easily.*

                   I think Augusta's more used to you than to me.

ANNIE   (*exiting*) Girl, her mother's the one that's been
                   there to feed her.

MARIA   (*to SARAH*) You were right to care for nothing
                   but your family.

SARAH   (*harshly*) No, Maria, I was wrong.

MARIA   It wasn't just the letter. When the rebellion began
                   I should have said ...we're about to have a child.
                   Nothing is as important as our staying together.
                   Instead I took the gun from the rack. I polished
                   it, I put it in Ben's hand. I cursed my luck that I
                   was pregnant and couldn't fight myself. For
                   what? For fiddlesticks.

SARAH   (*determined*) If Mackenzie were here today I'd be
                   the first one to join him.

MARIA   You'd be defeated too.

SARAH   Not before I shot the men who did this to us!

MARIA   Sarah, I finally understood why my father wouldn't pick up a gun. The only way to save a country is to kill all the people in it.

SARAH   (*meaning MARIA*) Not all the people.

LIZZIE   The hangman was nice...

MARIA   (*looking at baby in LIZZIE's arms*) And his children will go hungry because of it.

> *MARIA and LIZZIE freeze. SARAH rolls up her sleeves and adopts a practical tone.*

SARAH   (*to the audience*) So the weeks passed. My family lost everything, and took refuge with relatives. I told Mother I could support myself by housekeeping for Mrs. Beemer. (*kneeling and miming scrubbing the floor*) Lord knows there's enough dirt to keep me occupied.

> *ANNIE enters with a letter.*

ANNIE   That floor is as clean as it's ever going to be, girl. (*as SARAH keeps scrubbing, to MARIA*) This came for you.

MARIA   (*looking at it*) From Lord Durham.

ANNIE   Ain't you going to open it?

MARIA   What difference can it make?

SARAH   Maria! (*taking it and breaking the seal*) "Dear Mrs. Wait, I sail for England on the ship that brought the pigeons, that brought my recall...

> *DURHAM enters.*

DURHAM   (*overlapping*)...that brought my recall. If I could burn the boats and shoot the pigeons, I would do so for your sake, but even if I could, you would find that a new land is not a new world. Human

DURHAM (*continued*) nature is not changed by crossing an ocean. Tyranny and greed travel as far as we go, yet from this day on, as far as I go, your common sense will travel with me. So shall my notes for the report I was commissioned to write. (*as MARIA takes the letter from SARAH*) I shall try to keep working long enough to stop The Family Compact from gobbling up your dreams. And, my dear loving Maria, I shall endeavour to make our young Queen understand that if she must have colonies, and it would seem for now, she must, it might be rather nice, just once, once in the history of Empires, to try the simple but novel experiment of governing them well.

DURHAM exits.

MARIA (*revived*) I wonder if she'll listen?

SARAH I'm sure she will. He's her cousin.

MARIA I don't mean to him. I mean to me!

SARAH You want to go to England?

MARIA Durham can't plead for Ben as well as I can. I'll need money. Annie?

ANNIE What?

MARIA How much do you have left?

ANNIE What are you talking about?

MARIA I'm talking about Martin Overholt's thousand dollars.

ANNIE Sure the likes of you'll count no more than drops of dew to the Queen.

SARAH She counted to an Earl, didn't she?

MARIA You must want Jake home too?

ANNIE	I might be able to loan you a little bit...but you'll leave me the baby.
MARIA	Annie, I could be gone for years.
SARAH	It's all right. I'll look after them.
MARIA	You're coming with me. You have to teach me how to curtsey.
SARAH	I'm finished with curtseying. By the time we'd reach London, I'll be too big anyway.
MARIA	Oh, no...oh, Sarah, no.
SARAH	Don't worry about me, or Augusta...we'll be here for you whenever you get back.

LIZZIE brings AUGUSTA forward to MARIA who takes her, then passes her to SARAH.

SARAH	Maybe by the time our children grow up, there'll be a new world for them.
ANNIE	Girl, I doubt there's more to it than this.
MARIA	There will be, Annie! There has to be.

Blackout

The End.